The Eye Never Sleeps

Striking to the Heart of Zen

DENNIS GENPO MERZEL

Edited by Stephen Muho Proskauer

Introduction by
Hakuyu Taizan Maezumi

SHAMBHALA
Boston & London
1991

Shambhala Publications, Inc.
Horticultural Hall
300 Massachusetts Avenue
Boston, Massachusetts 02115

9 8 7 6 5 4 3

Printed in the United States of America on acid-free paper ⊚
Distributed in the United States by Random House, Inc., and
in Canada by Random House of Canada Ltd

Library of Congress Cataloging-in-Publication Data

Merzel, Dennis Genpo, 1944–
    The eye never sleeps: striking to the heart of Zen/Dennis
Genpo Merzel; edited by Stephen Muho Proskauer;
introduction by Hakuyu Taizan Maezumi.—1st ed.
        p. cm.
        ISBN 0-87773-569-7 (pbk.)
        1. Seng-ts'an, d. 606. Hsin hsin ming.
    2. Spiritual life (Zen Buddhism) I. Proskauer, Stephen Muho.
II. Title.
    BQ9288.S463M47 1991   90-52803
    294.3'4448—dc20   CIP

The Eye Never Sleeps

To Taizan Maezumi Roshi
with deepest gratitude and appreciation
for his continuous teaching and patience with me,
and to Brenda Hobai Liu,
with thanks for many years of love
and support.

If the eye never sleeps,
all dreams will naturally cease.
If the mind makes no discriminations,
the ten thousand things
are as they are, of single essence.
To understand the mystery of this One-essence
is to be released from all entanglements.

—*Sosan Zenji*

CONTENTS

EDITOR'S PREFACE

These fourteen Dharma talks on the ancient Chinese Zen poem *Hsin hsin ming* were given at *sesshins* (silent meditation retreats) in Holland and England by Genpo Sensei during the fall and winter of 1986. The first nine talks were published in two issues of the *Kanzeon Journal* during 1987 and 1988. Now the complete series is offered as a book so that others besides Kanzeon students may have the benefit of Genpo Sensei's clear and direct teaching.

Genpo Sensei gave a daily Dharma talk just before lunch. He began by reading a verse of the translated poem, then spoke extemporaneously, responding to the needs of the participants on that particular day. As you read, you can imagine you are sitting with Genpo Sensei as an involved retreat participant, listening to words being spoken for your own benefit.

As these talks are not scholarly discourses on the *Hsin hsin ming,* Genpo Sensei's teacher, Hakuyu Taizan Maezumi Roshi, abbot of the Zen Center of Los Angeles, has graciously contributed an introduction that gives the background of this ancient Chinese text. The translation by Richard B. Clarke, in a slightly modified version, is utilized throughout the book (with the kind permission of White Pine Press and the translator) and is printed in its entirety after the last talk.

While most of the Zen Buddhist terms used in the text are briefly defined where they first appear, a glossary will be found at the back of the book to assist the uninitiated reader. In the absence of a term of neutral gender to convey the meaning of both "esteemed leader" and "ancestor," the historical title *Patriarch* has been retained.

In preparing the talks for publication, it has been my intention to transform the spoken expression of the Buddhadharma into a written form that is compact and readable and also conveys the immediacy and power of the teacher's voice. This task is fulfilled when the printed language functions as a clear and open channel through which the teaching can flow freely, so that the receptive reader hardly notices the text itself.

My gratitude to Genpo Sensei for entrusting me with the editing of this book goes beyond words. I take full responsibility for and regret any distortions of his meaning that may have occurred in the process of transmutation from the spoken to the written medium.

Help from Catherine Genno Pages, Scott Daijo Springer, Hadea Munen Kriesberg, George Jisho Robertson, Monique Koren Vervecken, and many other Kanzeon students was vital to the creation of the manuscript. In a very real sense, the collective energy of everyone connected with the Kanzeon Sangha nurtured this book to completion.

Thanks also to Bonnie Myotai Treace of Zen Mountain Monastery for her encouragement and editorial suggestions.

We present these talks in deep gratitude to Genpo Sensei for his compassionate and patient teaching.

Stephen Muho Proskauer

ACKNOWLEDGMENTS

The author wishes to acknowledge White Pine Press and Richard B. Clarke for their kind permission to reprint a modified version of Clarke's translation of the *Hsin hsin ming* (New York: White Pine Press, 1984).

Thanks are also due to the Zen Center of Los Angeles for permission to use definitions from the glossaries of *On Zen Practice II* (Los Angeles: Zen Center of Los Angeles, 1976) and *The Hazy Moon of Enlightenment* (Los Angeles: Zen Center of Los Angeles, 1977), both edited by Hakuyu Taizan Maezumi and Bernard Tetsugen Glassman.

I am deeply grateful to the office staff of Kanzeon Zen Center and particularly to the editor of this book, Stephen Muho Proskauer, for many months of hard work putting my spoken words into a readable form. Without their energy and effort, this book would not exist.

Above all, I thank my esteemed teacher, Taizan Maezumi Roshi, who transplanted the Dharma to North America with total dedication and devotion. I am eternally indebted to him.

INTRODUCTION TO
THE HSIN HSIN MING

The famous *Hsin hsin ming* (Jap: *Shin jin mei*) is known as the first Zen poem. It consists of 146 four-word lines, directly and vividly expressing the Zen spirit in a simple, compact form. An outstanding characteristic of the poem is that it is written in genuine Chinese without using any Sanskrit or Pali Buddhist terms.

The main themes expressed in the *Hsin hsin ming* derive from *Two Entries and Four Acts*, one of the few authentic writings of the great Zen Patriarch Bodhidharma, who brought Buddhism from India to China in the sixth century. The roots of Bodhidharma's work can be traced to the *Vimalakirtinirdesa Sutra*, written sometime before the third century C.E. in India. Even though authorship of the *Hsin hsin ming* is traditionally attributed to the Third Patriarch, Chien-chih Seng-ts'an (Jap: Kanchi Sosan), the idioms employed in the poem have caused some scholars to place the date of its composition in a later year.

We have little information about the life of the Third Patriarch. His birthplace and birth date are unknown. According to the *Denko-roku* ("The Transmission of the Lamp"), written by Keizan Zenji (1268–1325), he was a layman over forty years old suffering from leprosy when he met the Second Patriarch, Hui-k'o (Jap: Eka), for the first time in 551 C.E. Being deeply impressed with this layman's capacity for the Dharma, Hui-k'o shaved the Third Patriarch's head and named him Seng-ts'an (Jewel of the Community). He was gradually cured of his illness and, after they had been practicing together for two years,

Hui-k'o gave him the robe and bowl signifying the transmission of the Dharma.

Anticipating the persecution of Buddhists in China prophesied by Bodhidharma, Hui-k'o ordered his successor to hide in the mountains and not to teach. The Third Patriarch remained in seclusion at Ch'ung-kung shan and Ssu-k'ung shan for over twenty-four years. He later met the monk Tao-hsin and transmitted the Dharma to him. After that, the Third Patriarch moved to Lo-fu shan, located northeast of Kung-tung (Canton), for three years. Then he returned to Ch'ung-kung shan and died there in 606 C.E. It is said that he passed away standing under a big tree with his palms together in *gassho*.

The title *Hsin hsin ming* is translated as *Verses on the Faith Mind*. The title of a poem is sometimes likened to the forehead, which expresses a person's unique characteristics. In *Hsin hsin ming*, *hsin* is generally understood as "faith." However, the word is also used in a different sense in the context of the verses, as, for example, at the very end:

> *Hsin hsin pu erh*
> Faith mind are not two
> *Pu erh hsin hsin*
> Nondual faith mind

The translator renders these lines as:

> *To live in this faith is the road to nonduality*
> *because the nondual is one with the trusting mind.*

In this context, *faith* does not have the usual meaning of "having faith in something," but rather that faith is the very *fact* of existence or reality itself. Dogen Zenji says, "Without attaining Buddhahood, the faith won't manifest. Where the faith manifests, Buddhas and Patriarchs manifest" (*Shobogenzo*). The *Nirvana Sutra* states, "Great faith is no other than Buddha nature." Kozan Garyu says that "one thousand seven hundred koans are all together the expression of this mind."

The word *ming* means "written expression" and also "warnings or admonitions," hence the title means "the verbal expression of the fact that the very nature of existence and of all the phenomenal world are no other than the faith mind." The *Hsin hsin ming* declares:

> *Although all dualities come from the one*
> *Do not be attached even to this One.*

That is to say, at the bottom of the two there is one and at the bottom of one there is zero. And that zero is "just this," the unborn one Mind, which is the faith mind.

From the time of its composition up to the present day, the *Hsin hsin ming* has been published and translated repeatedly by various scholars and appreciated by different Chinese and Japanese masters, who have written numerous commentaries on it. The masters' frequent references to the poem have authenticated it as a genuine expression of the spirit of Zen.

In the Sung dynasty, the verse *Hsin hsin ming nien-ku* of Chen-hsieh Ch'ing-liao (Jap: Shinketsu Seiryo, 1088–1151) was the first major commentary. Two centuries later, in the Yuan dynasty, Chung-feng Ming-pen (Jap: Chuho Myohun, 1263–1323) commented on the *Hsin hsin ming*. In 1667, during the Ming dynasty, Wei-lin (Jap: I Rin) wrote *Hsin hsin ming chu-yu* (Jap: *Jakugo*).

The founder of the Japanese Soto School, Dogen Zenji (1200–1253), quoted a number of passages from the *Hsin hsin ming* in his *Eihei-koroku*, written in Chinese. In 1303, Keizan Zenji, the cofounder of the Japanese Soto School, wrote the most famous Japanese commentaries on the verse, known as the *Hsin hsin ming nentei* ("*Teisho* on the *Hsin hsin ming*"). In 1781, during the Edo period, Kozan Garyu wrote a commentary, the *Hsin hsin ming yatosui*, which also contains Chen-hsieh Ch'ing-liao's verse and Keizan's *Nentei*. Rinzai master Isshi Benshu (1608–1646) also wrote a major commentary in Japanese entitled the *Hsin hsin ming benchu*.

In modern times, several Japanese commentaries have been written. Among the most famous are the commentaries by Kodo Sawaki Roshi on Keizan Zenji's *Hsin hsin ming nentei* and by Kodo Akino Roshi on Kozan Garyu's *Hsin hsin ming yatosui*. In addition, Ian Kishizawa Roshi has written the *Hsin hsin ming kattoshu*. D. T. Suzuki also gave concise, pithy comments on the *Hsin hsin ming*. The most recent commentary was written by Koun Yamada Roshi.

Genpo Sensei's interpretation of the spirit of the *Hsin hsin ming* is open and free, not restricted or conditioned by his predecessors' interpretations. I appreciate his vibrant expression, which I hope will give the reader encouragement and inspiration.

Hakuyu Taizan Maezumi
Los Angeles, California
February 1990

The Eye Never Sleeps

1 Have No Preferences

> The Great Way is not difficult
> for those who have no preferences.
> When love and hate are both absent
> everything becomes clear and undisguised.
> Make the smallest distinction, however,
> and heaven and earth are set infinitely apart.
> If you wish to see the truth
> then hold no opinions for or against anything.
> To set up what you like against what you dislike
> is the disease of the mind.
> When the deep meaning of things is not understood
> the mind's essential peace is disturbed to no avail.

It is so clear! Everything is stated right here in the first stanza, if we can only just realize it fully. The question is, can we take it? Can we see where we are holding preferences and how these preferences are forms of attachment? We know that attachment or clinging to self is the cause of suffering and confusion. Buddha's First Noble Truth—termed *noble* because it is beyond any question of true or false—is that *duhkha*, suffering or dissatisfaction, is the nature of existence. The Second Noble Truth declares that the cause of this suffering is attachment. Out of delusion and confusion arises self-clinging, our need to maintain the illusion of a separate self, or ego, which manifests in our forming preferences, in our picking and choosing. We hold on to all kinds of attachments: likes and dislikes, love and hate, passion and aggression.

What we generally call love, for instance, is quite often based upon attachment. We have certain ideas and pictures in our minds that go along with each of our relationships. When we say *my* husband, *my* wife, *my* parents, *my* child, a sense of possessiveness or ownership arises and, along with it, a set of expectations about how the other should be, as well as feelings of jealousy and fear of loss when we think the relationship is threatened. Thus, because of the concept of the relationship in our minds, we become attached, wanting to control and dominate the other. In this way we treat wives, husbands, parents, and children as less than human, reducing them to mere objects. We are expressing our attachment, not true unconditional love. Then we wonder why our relationships are not working, why we are dissatisfied and others are not happy with us.

Most of us want our children to outdo all the other children, to get the best grades in school and to do the best in athletics. Treating them thus, as extensions of our ego, is another expression of attachment. I used to get very frustrated with my father because his ego became so involved in my competitive swimming. He never got to compete himself because he had to start working at the age of ten. Even though he had always wanted to be involved in sports, he never had the chance; so I became an extension of him, a means to satisfy his unfulfilled desire.

Although I used to love swimming, I began to hate it because my father was always on my back, pushing me further, never giving me a day of rest. I would wake up at six o'clock every morning so I could work out from seven to eight before school. Then we would start again at two in the afternoon and go until six or seven at night. After dinner he would take me to the pool again from eight-thirty to ten-thirty. For twelve years I never took one day off! If there was a holiday and the pool where I trained was closed, we sometimes drove as far as fifty miles to a pool that was open.

By now, of course, I have learned to appreciate what tremendous discipline that was. I know it helped my sitting meditation practice later on, but there was a heavy price of resentment. When we try to live through our children, wanting them to be the greatest, we are clinging, using them to gratify our egos.

Maybe you are saying to yourselves, "Sure, I know people like that, but it doesn't apply to me." Stop now and take an honest look: see if you have any possessiveness, pride of ownership, tendency to compare, when you say *my* wife or *my* girl or *my* husband. How can we say someone is *mine, my* possession? What judgments, what rigid expectations, what needs of the ego lie behind that *my*? We ought to be aware and take note every time we think or talk that way.

This possessiveness does not satisfy us for long anyway. Some time ago I noticed how my young son, Tai, always wanted new toys. I wondered how long it would take him to realize that he grows tired of each new thing in just a few days. I bought him a Japanese car with a screen that showed the road. He could shift the gears to go faster and slower and even make it crash. He loved it for exactly three days.

I am just like that and you probably are, too. We are excited to get our new typewriter, our new computer, or our new television and, of course, we will continue to use them; but the thrill wears off. Everything that is new eventually becomes old. It is a natural law that whatever is born grows old and dies, ceases to exist; so we are constantly trying to get something new.

In America, this has become especially true even in our relationships with our spouses. We are ready to turn them in after a few years, after they have become a little worn out, a little shabby. They do not give us the same excitement. Almost everyone trades in their old cars and old television sets and even old houses for new ones. But although we always want new persons and things in our lives, at the same time we continue to cling to our same old preconceived notions about how they should be.

Our attachments may not only be to people and material objects. For instance, because of the emphasis on observing correct form during Zen retreats, some participants puff themselves up with pride at how well they perform the rituals and become very judgmental toward others. They think, Those people cannot do the form properly; they are fools, they are no good. Or the opposite may happen: we may become attached to the idea of "no-form" before we have even learned to do the rituals. We scoff at the forms, hold ourselves aloof from them, and think that those who seem attached to the rituals are fools. Now who is really the fool? Anyone who thinks the other is a fool! That is the only foolishness; other than that, there are no fools.

I once knew a person in high school who was considered a fool because when offered a choice between ten dollars and ten cents, he took the ten cents. The person who offered the money told everybody, "This guy is a fool!" Then someone else gave him the same choice and again he took the dime. I was very curious about what was going on. He cannot really be that stupid, I thought. So I asked him, "When these people offer you ten dollars or ten cents, why do you take the dime? Don't you realize ten dollars is worth a hundred times more than ten cents?" He replied, "If I took the ten dollars, they would never offer it again. This way I have collected much more than ten dollars. Everybody is offering me money. Everybody wants to see the fool."

The condition of our ego is visible not only in rituals but in everything we do. As we become more open, sensitive, receptive, there is less ego involved, and it shows. All of us are open books, completely transparent to anyone who is not caught up in himself, which means, of course, that hardly anybody notices us! We think people are watching us and we become very self-conscious and afraid. But most people do not see; they may look at us, but they do not really see us. They are too busy checking, wondering what we are thinking about *them*. Does he see through my facade, my mask? Does he see that I can barely hold it together, that I really don't know what this is all about, who I am, why I am here? Does he see that I am really nobody? That is what we really think—I am nobody. Then we try to prove we are somebody by attempting to control ourselves and others.

If you really look into your own mind, you will see through your ego. When Eka, who later became the Second Patriarch, came desperately to Bodhidharma saying, "My mind is not yet at peace," Bodhidharma replied, "Show me your mind! Where is this so-called mind that is not at rest?" He was using a beautiful tactic, *upaya* (skillful means), to make Eka turn his light inward. Eka searched ten days for his mind, sitting day and night, unmoving. You may laugh, thinking, How could it have taken him ten days? But most of us go on searching ten years or more, continuing to believe that *me* and *mine* really exist. We do not realize that the root cause of the problem is this *me* that we believe we have, that we think we are.

Finally Eka came back to face the great master Bodhidharma, who was over 115 years old at the time, with his big, mean, lidless eyes. At first, when Bodhidharma had said, "Show me this mind!" Eka had run away quivering, his tail between his legs. But after those ten days, Eka was transformed into a completely new man. Now, when Bodhidharma asked the question again, Eka answered truthfully: "I have searched everywhere for this mind and finally I have realized it is ungraspable, unattainable, unknowable." *It* cannot be seen, cannot be grasped. Why? Because the mind does not have a shape, it does not have a form, it is not a thing, it is a no-thing. It is vast and wide, boundless and limitless. That is why we say do not practice to gain something, because whatever you gain will turn to junk in your hands. Whatever you think you have you are not going to have forever. We try to grab hold of something, to have something to depend on, because the ground we stand on is very unsteady and feels like quicksand. It is even worse than quicksand; it is bottomless! The ground you are standing on does not exist; no wonder it feels so shaky. Let it go, cast away the mirage of the mind. Drop it completely!

Of course, you cannot willfully cast it away. You must allow it to drop off, but you have to first be willing to let it go. That is where intention comes in. Intention is not the same as having a goal. Intention is direction, and direction is most important. The intention must be to let go, to drop off body and mind. It cannot be your intention to hold on, to gain and accumulate, or you will never be able to do it. Only when your intention is clear, when you are just sitting without trying to get someplace or attain something in your practice, only then can you really let go of body and mind. Having the courage to look into your own mind, you realize: Aha! No mind. It is unsubstantial, it is not a fixed, solid thing. There is no self, no ego.

When we are first asked to find the thinker, we all say, "Obviously I am the thinker, I have all these thoughts. Who produces these thoughts but me?" But when we look more closely, we find ourselves wondering, "My God, where are these thoughts coming from? I don't know! They seem to be coming out of nowhere, out of empty space." They come like bubbles, rising up. They appear and then they disappear. Of course, we have preferences, so we suppress some of our thoughts; we don't like them. After we have been practicing for some time, we may stop rejecting some thoughts and cherishing others. How can we despise some of these thoughts, how can we pick some over others: "This bubble is better than that one," or "This is a bigger, prettier bubble"? Bubbles are bubbles; a thought is a thought. Why do we have such preferences about what thought pops up? We have no control over them anyway. Do you realize that? You have no control. You cannot control the thoughts that pop into your mind. They come from no place; they return to no place.

The same is true with our emotions. We think we have control over our feelings, but we do not. When we are sitting on our cushion, tears of sadness may flow. Why should we hate them and love joy? What is wrong with tears? To produce those tears is a natural function of the body and mind, a way of letting go, of cleansing or purifying.

Thoughts, sensations, emotions, even tears, are like the scenery that passes by. When you take a ride in the country, you just sit in the car and watch the scenery go by. You don't dwell on which parts you love and which you hate; you are just watching, not too interested or involved, yet paying attention. Be the impartial observer, like a mirror. Allow whatever comes to enter and, when it departs, just let it go, neither suppressing it nor attaching to it. If you think of it as a bubble, how can you get attached to it? It is only a bubble.

The same thing applies to your fantasies. Dogen Zenji, the founder of Japanese Soto Zen, never said, "Get rid of your fantasies." Yet we think, Oh, I should not be having this fantasy. What is wrong with a fantasy? Just watch it. The same with delusion: If I want to be enlightened, I should not be deluded. What is that? Just another preference. We prefer enlightenment over delusion. What is so great about enlightenment? It is not so great—maybe delusion is more fun! My teacher, Maezumi Roshi, always used to say, "I prefer to be deluded." I understand why now: it is much more fun, so naturally he preferred to be deluded.

In fact, if you choose to be deluded, since you are already deluded, then you are One, you are not in conflict any more, no longer split. If you think, I must become enlightened, it is obvious somewhere deep down you believe you are deluded. Since the deluded person is simply the one who believes he is deluded, then, when you are thinking you must attain enlightenment, you are the deluded fool! You are just deluding yourselves if you think: Oh, these great people, these great enlightened masters are so wonderful; but me, I am nobody, just a fool.

Choose to be deluded—it is easier! Be willing just to be in delusion; in fact, go one step further and really wish to be deluded, make a great effort to be deluded! Believe me, it comes very easily; you won't have to strive too long. Immediately, as soon as you choose to be deluded, it is already a given fact that you are enlightened. In our practice we hold no preferences. If delusion is there, fine! If enlightenment is there, that is also fine! After all, both delusion and enlightenment are only concepts. There is no delusion and no enlightenment. One who realizes this completely, with the whole being, is called "enlightened."

> *The Great Way is not difficult*
> *for those who have no preferences.*

Just begin to be aware in the moment when you are making preferences, such as "I do not like paying bills" or "I do not like cleaning house" or "I do not like rainy weather." The mind is extremely cunning. The easiest thing is to hold preferences, to form attachments. Begin to catch yourself; be aware when you are holding on to a preference. If you do not believe me (and I do not expect you to believe me), find out for yourself. Begin to observe what is happening around you and within you.

We think that so-called enlightened people are great because they seem to have such clarity. We think they are clever because they seem to know so much. But how did they get so clever? They started off like you and me, as ordinary people, but somehow they began to look into their own minds. Buddha himself did that; he was a great scientist. He saw there was a problem and he said to himself, I must look into the nature of suffering and find out what is the cause. He was very intelligent to begin with; he knew he was not going to find the answer "out there," so he looked inward. You are never going to find it outside, because the root of the problem is the mind.

When we look into our own minds and observe it, we begin to see that everything is impermanent, rising and falling, coming and going. Nothing is really static. Yet what are we always trying to do? To make everything stay put! We are trying to hold on, to feel safe and secure. The natural order of things is to flow like a river, but the flow is so fast, changing so quickly, that it feels unstable. There is nothing to hold on to, nothing we can depend on; it is moving too quickly. There is only one time when we will be safe and secure: in a pine box! Only then will you be secure; only there on your nice, soft bed, with your comfortable pillow. You will look good in there, too! You will be very, very secure when you are dead, but then it will be too late to enjoy life.

Don't you know life is insecure, life is a risk? The moment you were born, the risk of your death arose at the same time. That is why we say that life and death cannot be two things; you can never separate them. How can you have only life with never any death? With life comes the guarantee of death. The moment a child is born, death is inevitable.

But we go on clinging even though it is obvious that whatever we have is going to be lost, even our very lives. In fact, we tend to hold on all the more because we know we are going to lose. Then when we do lose what we were clinging to so strongly, sometimes we give up our lives, too. Often when a wife or husband dies, the partner dies soon after. Doctors and psychologists say that losing a child, a husband, a wife, or even a home, can trigger a terminal disease like cancer. If the survivors do go on living, they may remain so attached to the dead person that they stop enjoying life altogether.

Nothing is permanent. There is no safe and secure spot anywhere; we are all homeless. Only some of us realize it and some do not. When we see that we are truly homeless, sometimes we become monks, realizing this is our nature. Our true nature has no place to settle down, no resting place. In *shikantaza* ("just-sitting" Zen), we find no place to abide, because that is reality: there is no such place. We may as well face it: there is no place to stop. Yet we are always trying to sit down somewhere, attach to something, make ourselves secure and comfortable.

We do not like always moving in the river, so we dig a hole and make a tiny little pool along the edge to get out of the ceaseless flow. Can you see how your life is like that pool? Not a living pool, full of vital processes, cycles of new growth and decay, but completely stagnant: so sheltered and protected that it becomes static; the life goes out of it, the living thoughts and feelings die. Certainly it is safe and secure. We have built up the banks of the river around it, setting up barriers to make ourselves protected, so secure that life does not touch us, the flow of the river cannot reach us. Then we wonder why we do not feel we are really alive and fully functioning. We think, Why do I sometimes feel half-dead?

We have created such insulation between the whole of life and ourselves—not just a thin membrane, but a whole suit of armor—because we do not want to face impermanence and experience suffering, especially the suffering of others. There is such tremendous suffering and we do not want to be exposed to it, to feel that suffering ourselves. It is just too painful.

Because of our close connection with our parents, for instance, we have difficulty tolerating their anguish. I strongly resisted really experiencing my mother's pain about being left alone after my father's death. It was so deep—it seemed too much for me. I would insulate myself by falling into familiar roles with her. When I stepped out of these roles and allowed myself to get intimate with her pain, the relationship shifted. I am thankful for the three or four times when we have truly met as one mind. But most of the time I fall back into a familiar role and so does she. I walk through the door of her home and there is a wall between us. But sometimes, when we are alone, after three or four hours we drop the facade, we meet. It takes time, because we tend to play out the conditioned patterns first. And these patterns are not just in the mind—there are tensions in the body, too; body and mind are one. In zazen, we have the opportunity to drop our habitual ways of behaving by becoming aware of these patterns.

I used to live in a cabin in the mountains with no screens on the windows and doors and a bay window on one side. It was gorgeous to look out at the mountains, but birds would occasionally fly in through the door or windows and hit the glass wall of the bay window. Sometimes they were killed, but more often just stunned. If I got to the bird right away, picked it up and put it outside, the bird would recover. But if I did not get there before it revived, the bird would start flying around in a panic, going into a frenzy because it did not realize that the way out was the same as the way in.

The same door through which we enter is also the exit! What is this doorway? What does a baby have that brings him into this world? The urge to live, to be. When you do zazen, you step through this door and see: "Wow! There is a lot of space. It is just the way I have been perceiving things that kept me from experiencing that spaciousness." Our perspective shifts, it is no longer stuck in a fixed egocentric position.

In the beginning, all of us involved in Zen practice have the desire really to live, to be. We are trying to get somewhere, to be somebody. We have to pass through this stage of striving. Even though it may be an expression of ego, it is OK. Eventually, like a moth drawn to a flame, it will burn itself out. That is why when I say, "Expect nothing!", I do not really imagine that you will expect nothing. For a long time you are going to keep expecting something. I just want you to know the correct intention: expect nothing. The same thing that brings you in will bring you out. It is the same door. Just turn around.

But the poor bird won't turn around; it just keeps knocking against the glass wall. What a koan! Koans are just a means that we use to force you to keep banging your head against the glass, thinking it is the way out, and pretty soon, the glass gets thicker and thicker like an iron wall. Eventually there is a good possibility that you might just give up and turn around. There never was a wall, there never was a barrier. We created the barrier.

When love and hate are both absent
everything becomes clear and undisguised.

When you are no longer clinging, no longer loving in an attached way, a controlling way, nor having aversion toward things, then you can see things clearly as they are, without the observer. Then there is just seeing, just hearing. There is no one here, just space! The self is emptied of the self. When you are really empty and free of preferences, then everything is clear, undisguised. You begin to see through your own and others' masks.

That is what is so threatening when you see a Zen teacher in *daisan* (formal interview)—the fear that you are being seen through. Sure, the teacher sees through the mask, but there is no judgment about it. That is why you are there. That is what interview is for: to drop the mask, to drop the separation that never was there to begin with. We put it there to protect ourselves. If we drop the protection, become one mind, then teacher becomes student and student becomes teacher. Then we realize: Ah, all along I was the master, not him. I just thought he was. He is only what I have to go through, he is the doorway to realizing I am the true master.

For years I resisted surrendering to Maezumi Roshi. He was not perfect. In fact, he seemed quite imperfect! And yet it finally looked like I had to surrender to him. I had so many reasons not to do so, but when it happened, do you know what it was, in truth? The self surrendering to the self, Buddha to Buddha! Only Buddha becomes one with Buddha. When you let go, when you surrender, what you discover is yourself, you find your true self, your real self, you find the master, you find the Buddha. Then you do not have to pretend to be somebody, because now you know who you are, what you are. You have great faith in yourself. You do not have to be someone special. You do not have to get into politics to prove you have power. You no longer have to have control over your wife or your kids, because you truly know who you are. And yet what that is can never be expressed.

What is your true self? It will forever be a mystery, because it is ungraspable and unknowable. Though it is beyond all labels and words, forever unnameable, we give true self all kinds of names: Mind, Buddha, true nature, original face. They are just labels. When you experience true self, you just experience it. There is no one there experiencing it; there is just *it*. Then the sky is blue, the clouds are white, valleys are low, and mountains are high.

Make the smallest distinction, however,
and heaven and earth are set infinitely apart.

During the first formal interview I had with Maezumi Roshi, he asked, "Are you vegetarian by any chance?" I replied proudly, "I never eat meat!" He said, "Do not be attached to any ideology, any belief." I thought, Ah, surprise! *That* is Zen. Do not be attached to anything! Of course, there is nothing wrong with being a vegetarian, but I was using this choice to support an image of myself as super-spiritual. Roshi could easily see that my being a strict vegetarian had become a big point of ego-attachment for me and he wasted no time in making me conscious of my spiritual arrogance.

When I left Roshi's interview room that first time I said to myself, "Here is a man who kills Buddhas." I was a Buddha, I knew that. I went in there as a Buddha, to have Dharma combat, thinking, I am enlightened. I am the clearest Buddha who ever walked this earth. How could he think he is the best? And he killed me in one jab! Of course, it took years for me to let go completely.

We hold on to our ideologies, to our delusions. Look into yourself and see if you feel free; maybe you are still attached to beliefs and ideologies. I am not saying: "No rules." I am only saying to respond appropriately, freely. Freedom is lost if you are trapped in the rules, but it is also lost if you are conditioned to rebel and caught up in always challenging the rules.

We all become addicted to strange beliefs like, "Buddha said such-and-such." How many know what Buddha said? Is there anybody who knows what Buddha really said? Even the scholars do not agree on that. And who is this Buddha anyway? You are. That is what you have to realize without a shadow of a doubt. You are the Buddha, not some historical Buddha who lived twenty-five hundred years ago. You are the master! Do not be conditioned by anything.

> *If you wish to see the truth*
> *then hold no opinions for or against anything.*

If you wish to see the truth, you must indeed hold no opinion for or against anything. "I do not like this, I like that; that is no good, this is good." Be like water, be fluid. When it is a round container, be round; when it is a square container, be square. Be at home, be at ease in any situation. When it is formal, be at ease in the formal situation; when it is informal, be at ease in the informal situation. Some of you may be at home among the hippies, but you cannot be with politicians. Wherever you are, be at home.

What kind of freedom do you have if you can only be at ease when you are alone? I spent one year in a cabin, comfortably alone, but the moment I went out, the world was too much. I retreated right back to my cabin. It took me one year in the middle of Los Angeles to get over my attachment to being at peace alone in a cabin. In Los Angeles when we sat, sometimes there were gunfights going on around us, loud radios blasting Mexican music outside the windows, even people getting killed on the street. You have to be able to sit right in the midst of your busy life. What good is it if you can sit only beside the stream or in your room or in a closet?

> *To set up what you like against what you dislike*
> *is the disease of the mind.*

This is the root of the problem: the mind, always setting up likes against dislikes, what we approve of against what we disapprove of. We put the blame out there, as if we were victims. This is even reflected in the zazen posture. If we slump, sitting as though we were carrying the world on our shoulders, we are making ourselves victims in life. Everything is too heavy; life is just too much and we want to escape. There are many forms of escape. Zazen can be one of them, or going off into the mountains, or dying of cancer. We can choose even to commit suicide, consciously or unconsciously.

But when you sit with dignity, you feel like paying attention, you feel like loving, like giving, like being generous, because you are the king, you are the Buddha. You are not some slave, but the true master! When the ego thinks it is the master, the true master is absent and you become the slave to the ego, to all kinds of desires, attachments, likes, and dislikes; but when you take the posture and sit up straight, you find your true self. The true master comes back into the house: "Oh, I have been gone a long time. What has happened here? Good things, bad things; it is all a mess. Let's clean up the room, make the bed, set things straight. Let's appreciate each other a little more, love each other, be a little kinder. I have been so closed in, so confined, so imprisoned, I didn't have time to appreciate you."

> *When the deep meaning of things is not understood,*
> *the mind's essential peace is disturbed to no avail.*

Peace is our natural state of mind, clarity is our natural state of being. It is like a jar of water in which the impurities have settled: the water is clear. That is our natural state: that rest, that peace, that clarity. But we are always shaking the jar with our likes and dislikes, preferences, fears, and upsets; then the water becomes cloudy. Though it is unnatural, that is the state in which we survive, somewhere between death and life, in a semicoma, just barely functioning.

What are we to do? Drop the mind. How? See into it. Dogen Zenji said that the *bodhi*-mind, the awakened mind, is that which sees the constant arising and falling away of all things. So simple.

When you sit up straight, taking the posture, you can begin to see the nature of all phenomena, of all things. It is all empty: not void, but empty-infinite, constantly in flux, constantly changing. It is not fixed and solid, it is unsubstantial. This body is unsubstantial, all things are unsubstantial. Just observing the arising and dissolving of things *is bodhi*-mind.

2 *Serene in the Oneness of Things*

The Way is perfect like vast space
where nothing is lacking and nothing is in excess.
Indeed, it is due to our choosing to accept or reject
that we do not see the true nature of things.
Live neither in the entanglements of outer things,
nor in the inner feeling of emptiness.
Be serene in the oneness of things
and such erroneous views will disappear by themselves.
When you try to stop activity to achieve passivity
your very effort fills you with activity.
As long as you remain in one extreme or the other,
you will never know Oneness.

The Way refers to the Tao, the order of the universe. The Tao, the Way as it is, before the mind interferes, is in perfect order; the Tao is just what it is. When we sit in zazen and we just allow everything to be as it is without acceptance or rejection, without liking or disliking, without approving or disapproving of the way things are, they are already in perfect harmony. But our rational, dualistic mind just cannot perceive that; it is simply impossible.

We are like a lake that has been churned up by the wind, very turbulent and murky. We cannot simply see things as they are in their perfect order because the muddy water, like a mirror covered with dust, cannot reflect things clearly. When we sit and settle ourselves down, when all the mud settles to the bottom, then the water becomes crystal clear and the surface becomes a smooth mirror reflecting the whole just as it is. But as long as the wind of discursive thought is stirring up the mind, making ripples on the water, the whole is fragmented and we cannot see the unity of all things.

Our dualistic mind causes this fragmentation, the inability to see the Way perfect as it is in its natural state. Dualistic consciousness is created by the thinking mind. A random thought that rises like a bubble to the surface of the water is no problem. Even random thought after random thought after random thought is no problem. In water, bubbles naturally arise; in the ocean, waves naturally appear. So, too, the natural functioning of the mind is to generate thoughts. By themselves, they are not the problem, but when we put these thoughts together, combining them into a continuous flow, we create the illusion that there is a self, a *me*. Out of this comes the concept that I exist as a separate entity apart from the whole: there is a *me* in the world looking out at the world.

This concept of a separate self is the fragmentation. Because of this, the surface of the water is no longer smooth; the mirror is broken up and cannot reflect the whole. The full moon may be shining in the sky, but the whole image is not reflected; we see only patches of light. Likewise, our true nature is always present, but we only recognize fragments. We cannot realize it in its totality even though our true nature is always manifesting.

The true nature of all things is continuously manifesting. When a dog barks or pees on the ground, that dog's true nature is in realization. The dog is manifesting dog nature, just as a stick lying on the ground manifests its stick nature. All things are always manifesting their true nature. We never look out at a tree and say, "That tree is imperfect, that tree is not manifesting its true nature." We only look at ourselves and other human beings and say, "We are not manifesting our true nature."

Why do we say that? Because when it comes to humans, we have an idea of what it is to be saintlike, to be a perfected human being. We don't realize that each human being is always manifesting his true nature, no matter what that person is doing. It is that simple! As a human being, you cannot do anything but manifest your true nature. But we have the dumb idea, the dualistic notion, that we must be special, we must be saintlike, we must be perfect in order to manifest our true nature, and so we work diligently at becoming perfect. As long as we approach it in this dualistic way, we can never become perfect.

It is like the Chinese yin/yang symbol: within the perfect is going to be the imperfect and within the imperfect is going to be the perfect. There is a story about a monk who was raking leaves in the rock garden. Not a leaf or twig was out of place, but still something was not quite right. He knew that, but he could not figure out what the problem was. He kept looking at the rock garden, seeing it was not just so. When the master came out, the monk said to him, "You know, I have worked for hours on this rock garden and still it is not perfect." The master took one glance, walked over, and shook a tree. Some leaves scattered on the ground and the monk said, "Ah!"

There has to be that imperfection within the perfection for it to be perfect. In other words, we cannot be literally "perfect." There is no such thing as a perfect saint, really. If we could get into a saint's mind, we would find the sinner. Looking into the dreams and fantasies of a saintly person, you encounter all kinds of sins. What it means when we try so hard to be saints is that we are repressing, disowning the sinner within us. But every one of us has the sinner and every sinner has the saint. If you go into a sinner's dream, you know what you find? The wish to be a saint! The sinner dreams of being perfect, of doing good things. Although he cannot seem to act saintly, still the sinner's thoughts are about being perfect; while the so-called perfected one, the saint, is having all kinds of aggressive and erotic fantasies.

Those who try hard to be saintly sometimes come in to interview and tell me, "Oh, I am having such sexual fantasies!" Why? Because an intensive meditation retreat brings up whatever we are repressing. What we are disowning, the sinner in us, is going to come up when we open to ourselves. That is why Suzuki Roshi said, "I'd rather tell my students to be a little bit naughty." I never tell students, "Don't do that! Be this! Be that!" because the moment we try to be something really good, outwardly we may succeed, but inwardly we are in chaos, confusion. We are not really settled within ourselves, not really in harmony, not really at home, because we are suppressing so much.

This has happened to me throughout my practice. I noticed that when I was suppressing my sexual urges or my anger or my jealousy, all my dreams and wishes were to be more sexual or more angry or more jealous. In an even more suppressed and more subtle way I got angry inwardly but didn't recognize it. Then I hated the person who was able to get angry: "How come that person is always so angry, so jealous?"

For years, it used to bother me that my wife liked to criticize and judge other people. Not only my wife but also my previous girlfriends seemed very critical. *I*, of course, never judged or criticized like that! One day, while working on this issue, I realized I had been suppressing the judge in me. As a spiritual person, a Zen monk, I thought one should not judge others, so I had completely disowned that part of myself. When that really became clear to me, all the energy bound up in my suppressed judgments was suddenly released. Several weeks later, my wife said to me, "Have you noticed that I am judging less?" She was right. She no longer was needing to express what I had been disowning.

In our relationships, if we see something in our partner that really bothers us, we had better look for how we are suppressing it in ourselves, how we are not owning that aspect, making ourselves incomplete. When we deny or suppress these various parts of ourselves, we cannot experience our wholeness.

Shikantaza is just being that space, allowing the space for everything to be what it is. It is so simple, just to be what we are; it is creating tremendous space. In Japanese, the word for hell means "no space." When we leave no space for ourselves, we are in hell; and when we leave no space for others around us, they are in hell. In our relationships, when we cannot allow the other space, the other is going to feel suppressed and will eventually get upset, reacting to us by becoming possessive and demanding, for example.

Take a look at yourself to see what you are suppressing. I just realized recently—and we continuously realize things; it never ends—that I have been suppressing the one who tries to do things perfectly. I have been saying for years, "Don't try to be perfect." It always bothered me when I saw people trying to be perfect; they seemed so uptight. I just disowned that part of myself that wants to do things perfectly because I felt it was wrong.

There was one monk I met in Japan who tried to do everything perfectly. He was a very stiff person but very strong, too. I kept looking at him; I liked him, but something about him kept bothering me. Every time we came back into the room, he would fold all his clothes very precisely in a cloth and put them away neatly. His suitcase looked immaculate, in perfect order. The rest of us were just folding things casually and throwing them in. I started to realize how I had been rejecting perfectionism in myself because it looked too stiff and unnatural, and my way was to be natural.

Certainly, the perfect way can be loose and natural; but this need not exclude doing things correctly or being mindful or attentive to how we fold our clothes. We can easily say, "Oh, this guy is very attached to doing things perfectly," but our judgment may really be a rejection of part of ourselves and an attachment to being casual or sloppy. If so, instead of judging the other person, we can come home again, take a good look at ourselves, and see how identified we are with doing things improperly and imperfectly.

> *The Way is perfect like vast space*
> *where nothing is lacking and nothing is in excess.*

Don't think of the Way as something outside yourself, as something apart from your mind. When you just sit in zazen, the mind is like vast space with no outside perimeter, no circumference. The mirror has no edge and no stand; there is no outside to this mind. Pointing to the body you say, "This mind." You cannot separate mind and body. Mind and body have no end, no limit, no boundary.

We all experience energy and the movement of that energy in our zazen, but we do not always realize that there is no outer limit to the energy flow. It radiates out in unbounded concentric circles much like waves when a stone is dropped into a body of water. The benefits of the positive energy generated in our zazen penetrate the entire world in a very real sense, but invisibly. When you begin to sit well, you start feeling this energy in the body as the power of *samadhi* (one-pointed attention) arises. Don't let someone who has never sat and experienced this tell you it is impossible, that there is no way a human being can create such energy. You can verify it by your own experience when energy is produced in your zazen.

And if we believe that energy is locked in the physical body, in this bag of skin, and does not flow outward as well as inward, then we have fallen into a certain kind of arrogance. Why do we suppose that we are the only one experiencing this heat, this joy, this serenity, this peace? How can there be any end to this energy? Why do we assume that it stops anyplace? How could we have the audacity to think that it is only experienced within the boundary of our own skin? Maybe because the consequences, when we begin to reflect on them, are almost too much for us: every single event, whether it be thought or word or act, is producing and directing energy. It is only our arrogant, deluded mind that believes it stops with us. It does not stop at the skin, it does not stop at the door of this room, it does not stop at the borders of this country, and it does not stop at the outer edge of our atmosphere. Every event ripples out forever in all ten directions, throughout space and time, because there is only here and only now. All past and future are now; all places in the universe are here.

There was once a monk, Hyakujo, who was walking with his master, Baso. Baso saw birds flying by and said, "Where have they gone?" Hyakujo replied, "They have flown away." Baso grabbed Hyakujo's nose and twisted it really hard. Hyakujo shouted out, "Ouch! What are you doing?" Baso wanted him to see the true situation! Where could the birds have gone? Is there any place to go? Any place to hide? Any place that is not home?

As monks, we are supposed to be homeless, having left our homes behind; but once we are homeless we realize that every place is home; wherever we happen to be is our home. This planet is our home; if we go to the moon, that is our home. We cannot leave home. It is a paradox: when there is no fixed abode, no fixed home, every place is home. It works the same way with our minds. If the only place we feel at home is within our own prejudices and opinions and ideas, then our minds are fixated, stuck. Then we feel at home and friendly only with people who agree with our philosophy. We seek out people who have the same views and avoid those who hold different views because we feel uncomfortable with them.

A man I know and his brother have not spoken one word to each other in ten years. Why? Because there is one philosophical point over which they disagree. My friend installs nuclear power plants around the world and his brother is antinuclear. Here is a man in favor of world harmony and peace—and it may indeed be a wonderful thing to be against nuclear power and nuclear bombs—but the moment he says, "I am against," he has taken a fixed position and become stuck. Now we are against everybody who is in favor. Even two brothers are at war and cannot enter the same house, all for such a righteous notion. "I am against nuclear power plants, I am against nuclear bombs, so I am against my brother. I can never be at peace with my brother." If you stop to think about it, this is utterly stupid. But we don't stop to think. We can see it in others, but when it comes to our own opinions, we are so nearsighted.

The ones who are against create the ones who are for. There must be the two opposed camps for there to be conflict. In karate practice, when we start doing freestyle I notice all the less experienced students are in constant conflict, blocking or attacking, the only two things they know. The more experienced and really capable students know how to retreat; they step back out of the way leaving nobody for their opponent to fight, nobody to offer resistance.

I remember once, a person who was in charge of publishing one of Maezumi Roshi's books told him, "I would like to print ten thousand copies of this book." Roshi said, "Fine, do as you will." But then this editor went on, "I am not sure, ten thousand may be too small a number, maybe we should print twenty thousand." Roshi replied, "Fine, do as you wish." The man then said, "But I am not sure this book is any good, maybe we should not print it at all." Roshi said, "Fine, so do whatever you want." The editor said, "But it has the possibility of being a coffee-table best-seller and we might even sell thirty thousand!" "Fine," Roshi said, "do as you will." Then the editor started thinking, "This man is not taking a position; I am going to force him to take a position." So he started saying outrageous things, and the more he said, the more there was just nobody out there taking a stand. Pretty soon he had to give up in complete frustration because there was no opposition.

We are always opposed to something, always for or against; we are taught that in school. You have to have an opinion, you have to like or dislike. When you go to the museum, you are expected to express your opinion: "This is a wonderful painting, a great painting. Oh, but look at that terrible one over there!" You can't just look at the painting, holding no opinion. What happens when you give up all these opinions and your profession is art? Everything is a perfect painting. And, in a way, this is true, isn't it? Every tree is a perfect tree. Nature does not make some trees perfect and other trees imperfect. The same thing with paintings. We can say some trees or paintings are more perfect, but only from a relative standpoint. Human beings certainly appear different: some more saintly, some born crippled, some without much intelligence, some crazy, but who is to say which is more perfect?

When I used to work with emotionally disturbed children, I saw how some of them could throw themselves more completely into whatever they were doing than most of us can. They were less concerned over how they appeared and what others thought about them. They just were totally caught up in whatever they did. The rest of us are too clever and controlled and sophisticated to be like that.

In the time of the Buddha there was once a very unclever monk who wanted to see the Buddha face-to-face; but the monks around the Buddha said, "You can't see him; you are too stupid." The unclever monk said, "But I want to attain the fourth level of arhatship!" The monks said, "Then you don't need to see the Buddha. We will help you." They told him to go sit in the corner, facing the wall. Like the innocent idiot he was, he went and did what he was told. The monks threw a coconut at him, hitting him on the head. "Ouch! What have you done?" "You have just attained the first level of arhatship," the monks replied. "Now go and sit in the second corner." When he did, they picked up another coconut and hit him on the head again. "Ouch!" "You just attained the second level of arhatship," said the monks. "Go and sit in the third corner now." Then they hit him with coconuts in the third and fourth corners. Afterward the unclever monk ran to them, made three bows in front of them and walked away as a Buddha! But those clever monks are still sitting there, wondering what happened, still trying, struggling, knowing full well that they are not there yet.

Mumon said, "Not knowing is most intimate." To go beyond both knowing and not knowing is most intimate: to be simply at one with it. How is it that we split ourselves, that we do not feel at one? Because we know too much; we have too much knowledge, too much understanding, and too much information. We are too clever. Maybe we are graduates from the university or professors or doctors or painters. All that learning keeps us from being really intimate.

If we just forget it all, if we drop the mind, then there is only the experience itself. When you are sitting and there is a sudden clap of thunder and suddenly you have forgotten all you know, isn't it beautiful? Isn't it wonderful? Mind has dropped off and everything is as it is! Everything is in perfect order when we let go of all our knowledge, when we drop the mind, when we forget the self.

Some students come to me saying, "I just can't make the leap, I can't let go." Why? Because they are too clever, they know too much; they know everything beforehand and understand it all. They read too much. I love working with the karate people, because they don't know anything about Zen or spirituality. They have never been interested, they just want to fight, be able to defend themselves. They want to be tough; they want to control their lives. They don't want to be frightened anymore when they walk the streets, so they come to study karate. They start to feel more confident, facing themselves more, but they are not interested in all that spiritual stuff. When you work with them they are not bringing along a tremendous amount of information and knowledge. They just want to know the most simple things: How do I greet my opponent? How do I hold my legs? How do I line up correctly? How is my posture supposed to be? What should I do with my mind? The questions are always so simple, so direct and to the point. If I start getting intellectual or conceptual, they say, "Wait a minute, just show me how to sit, how to breathe, how to concentrate. I don't want to know all the other business."

Indeed, it is due to our choosing to accept or reject
that we do not see the true nature of things.

When I go to Poland to teach, a constant flow of people come to visit me. Someone once said to me there, "It has been amazing to watch what happens in your room. You don't reject anybody. Whoever walks in, you sit down with him and talk to him, give him tea and chat until he leaves. I could not stand some of them. How can you be so kind and nice to this one or that one?"

If in our sitting we are constantly rejecting certain feelings, certain thoughts, certain emotions, certain ideas, and are clinging to those that we call creative, wonderful, or beautiful, then also in our life we are going to be doing exactly the same thing. We will like certain people, clinging and attaching to them, while despising and rejecting others. But when we become like vast space, there is no picking and choosing. Everyone is equal, everyone is just a reflection of ourselves and we can begin to appreciate the different qualities in each person, the beauty in each one.

Everyone, even the most ugly person, has some beauty, some wonderful qualities, and likewise every beauty has something ugly about it. All you have to do is begin to live with someone and you will find it. Everybody farts, everybody shits, everybody smells. There is a story about a woman who brought home two monkeys and a dog and wanted them to live in her bedroom. Her husband objected, saying, "But dear, what about the smell?" She replied, "Don't worry about the smell. I got used to it; they will get used to it, too!"

> *Live neither in the entanglements of outer things,*
> *nor in the inner feeling of emptiness.*

Don't live entangled with external things. Don't get drawn out of yourself and attached. If we hear beautiful sounds, right away our attention gets pulled out toward them. Our dualistic mind enters and we start liking or disliking: "Oh, that's beautiful music!", "Oh, that's a beautiful painting!", or "That's so ugly!" It can happen through any of our senses: through seeing, hearing, feeling, thinking. For instance, why are we so attached to sex? Because it feels good and we become attached to that feeling or to the memory of that feeling. Even after it stops feeling so good we remain caught up in it, like a rat that has been trained to go through a maze to get a reward. We get all wrapped up in habitual patterns, the vines and entanglements of the senses, losing our true selves.

Likewise we may become attached to an inner feeling, such as emptiness, and then we seek it over and over again: I want more of this peace. I am going to do a longer retreat, sit even stronger, in order to have more of these good feelings. And that very striving to get more is exactly what keeps us from really being at peace, from truly being at rest, at ease. The seeking itself is the problem.

> *Be serene in the oneness of things*
> *and such erroneous views will disappear by themselves.*

Be at peace with the way things are. In the natural state of things we are already at one. Because your natural mind is already one, when you try to become one, when you try to get someplace or gain something, you have already gone astray. By the very effort to become one you have already missed. Why is it so difficult just to sit up straight and be natural? Why is it so difficult to sit here and do nothing, to seek after nothing? "It is very boring. I am not accomplishing anything. I have nothing to show for my efforts. I am wasting my time!"

We must not waste our time. We chant that in our sutra "Identity of Relative and Absolute": "Do not waste your time by night or day." You know how we are really wasting our time? By running after things, the opposite of what we usually say. "When I sit and do nothing I am wasting my time" is an upside-down view of life. "Don't waste your time by night or day" means don't keep running after everything, trying to accumulate more.

In Zen practice, to gain is to lose, to lose is to gain. To let everything go is to gain it all. If I grab hold of a rose bush, the thorns may hurt my hands, but at least this pain is something known, familiar. Familiarity somehow makes me feel comfortable, even though I am in pain and suffering. My life feels secure even if it is not working. Security is what we want more than anything. A known quantity, even a false sense of security, is more comfortable than facing the truth of our insecurity.

When we finally face the truth and let go of our fear, we are filled up with the Dharma. Just open your hand and you are filled with it! It takes a lot of energy to keep your hand clenched, but if you relax and let go, the hand naturally opens by itself, just like a rose. It actually requires more effort on your part to keep yourself closed than to open up. Five hours' sleep might be enough for most of us, were it not that it requires so much energy to stay in control, to hold it all together. Just let go! But if you ask how, I cannot tell you. No one can tell you how to let go.

When my son was learning to swim, I would say, "OK, Tai, jump into the pool, jump!" And he would sit there at the edge of the pool and say, "OK, Daddy, I will."

"Tai, jump now!"

"OK, Daddy, I will, I am trying! I am trying, Daddy, I am trying *hard*, Daddy. I'll do it, I am really trying to let go and just dive in."

"Come on, Tai, dive, jump!"

"I will . . . tomorrow. Tomorrow I'll do it."

When will he do it? What is still required? Obviously, trust. He has to trust me, he has to trust the water, and he has to trust himself. You are not going to jump, you are not going to take the leap until, first of all, you trust yourself that it is really going to be all right. When you really make that jump, it looks like one hundred feet down. We have the koan: How do you take the next step from a hundred-foot pole? It looks like you are falling into an abyss, that you are going to lose your life, because the only life that you know is the personal one, the small one, the limited one. When you jump, it is really just the next step, but you can't know that, you can't possibly know that until you jump. You can hear me saying it a million times, but you can't know until you trust yourself and me and the process enough to jump. The water is going to hold you up. Even if you go down, you are going to bounce right back up. The universe will support you.

When you jump like that, the only thing you ever lose is your personal identity, your ego. What you find is your true life, your real life, the one that has no limit, the one that does not feel constricted and confined. What you find is tremendous space, freedom, liberation, peace. All that effort to hold on has bound you up into a tight little ball of rigid ideas and opinions. Who can live with all that? Who wants to be around someone so closed, opinionated, antagonistic, easily angered, and upset?

But we go on clinging for dear life to what we know, to what we see as secure and safe. We walk up one hundred and one times to the precipice and say, "Some other time!", until one day we feel enough faith in ourselves to jump. At that moment we see that we are not lacking anything. We already have it. We have always had the faith required to make the leap. How can we really believe that the true mind, the true self, has ever been lacking in anything at all? What can be missing? It is a whole, a totality. Only the restricted egocentric self feels as if something is missing. And for the ego it is true: life, our very life itself, is missing! When we go beyond the ego and experience the sudden revelation that absolutely nothing is lacking, then immediately the faith is there to jump. The leap itself is the revelation, the revelation is the leap.

But somehow we want assurance beforehand: "Guarantee me it is going to be OK, that I am not going to lose my wife, my car, my garden, my home, sex, drinking, all the things that I enjoy and that tell me who I am!" We want some guarantee, but all I can tell you is that to lose is to win. When you drop everything, you gain everything. There is no shortage. You will have more offers than you know what to do with! That will be the next problem. There will be an abundance of everything and how to handle that is going to be the next stage of practice.

When you merge with the whole vast, deep ocean, when you are no longer identified with the waves on the surface, there is nothing lacking. As long as you identify with the waves, your life is constantly going up and down. When you are one with the ocean, there are no longer any ups and downs. Everything deepens and evens out. Every day is a good day. Every day is a perfect day.

When you try to stop activity to achieve passivity
your very effort fills you with activity.

The very effort to stop the ceaseless movement of thoughts keeps us stirred up. Just give up all this effort to stop thinking! Fruitful effort is to let go of effort. Strive to stop striving! When you do, everything settles by itself. Body and mind drop off naturally in time, just as an apple falls when it is ripe. If you pick it too soon, it is still green, like some of us who pass many koans but remain immature in practice. Everything, everyone ripens in their own time. Don't rush things. Let them unfold; let them evolve naturally.

As long as you remain in one extreme or the other,
you will never know Oneness.

As long as you are caught up in accepting or rejecting, liking or disliking, you can't know true peace, true oneness. Even though you are constantly at one, all dualities create separation in your mind and you don't realize the oneness that you are.

3 *Return to the Root*

Those who do not live in the single Way
fail in both activity and in passivity,
assertion and denial.
To deny the reality of things
is to miss their reality;
to assert the emptiness of things
is to miss their reality.
The more you talk and think about it,
the further astray you wander from the truth.
Stop talking and thinking
and there is nothing you will not be able to know.
To return to the root is to find the meaning,
but to pursue appearances is to miss the source.
At the moment of inner enlightenment,
there is a going beyond appearance and emptiness.
The changes that appear to occur in the empty world
we call real only because of our ignorance.
Do not search for the truth;
only cease to cherish opinions.

When we talk about Truth with a capital *T*, meaning the absolute Truth, then there can be only one Truth, only one Way; and that one Way can be found in all religions and practices. This statement may offend some people unless it is clearly understood.

On the relative level, of course, there are many truths with small *t*. But when we reach the summit and have that true experience, which is what Zen is really about, then we know there can be only one Truth and it is the same for whoever realizes it: from whatever culture, whatever religion, whatever background, whether male or female, young or old, Chinese, Japanese, Indian, English, Dutch, or American. The Truth is universal, sometimes called Emptiness, or God.

What is the Truth? In a way we can say that's what our practice is, to realize, or to attain the Truth. And what, then, is the best way for us to find this Truth? Obviously if we are searching for it outside ourselves, we can never reach it. Unfortunately, most people don't even realize this and continue to seek for the Truth in the phenomenal world, in external things, thinking that they are going to reach some kind of ultimate happiness or peace by accumulating possessions, power, wealth, fame, position, and so forth. But not very much is required, only a slight shift in perspective, to see that we can never reach *it* by the arrow pointing outward.

There is nothing more wonderful for me than to hear my students give talks that point the arrow inward and manifest the Dharma right before my eyes. I start to believe, "Maybe it works! Maybe this dumb practice really does work!" Sometimes I have my doubts: interview after interview, watching us being so preoccupied, so self-involved, hardly seeing past our own noses. Sometimes I have to wonder, does it really work? But then come the days when I see students becoming empty vessels and the Dharma just flowing out of them!

There is a koan about two of my favorite characters, Ganto and Seppo. Ganto was about five years younger than Seppo, but his own realization happened earlier and was very clear. Ganto had studied under Tokusan, who was also a great master. Tokusan was famous for being a very strict, tough teacher. He is particularly noted for one particular koan: every time anyone came into interview with him, he would shout, "Say a word of Zen!" and no matter what the student said or did, he would hit him about thirty times with his stick and then kick him out.! He was a big man and really stern.

Late in his life, Tokusan became much gentler. We have another koan that shows this. One day Seppo saw Tokusan heading down the corridor toward the dining room for the informal evening meal. Seppo was the *tenzo*, the chief cook, and even today in Rinzai monasteries the kitchen is called *seppo ryo*, Seppo's room. In a Zen monastery, when it is time to eat, the bell is hit and there are three rounds on the drum to summon the abbot after everybody else has assembled. Seeing Tokusan coming, Seppo said, "Old Master, the bell has not been rung and the drum has not been struck. Where are you going with your bowls?"

Seppo was then forty-one years old, just a youngster, and Tokusan was about eighty. Here is tough Tokusan—monks used to be frightened to death to go into interview because they knew whatever they did or said, they were just going to get beaten— and Seppo had the gall to say something like, "Hey, old man, what are *you* doing out here? It is not time for dinner yet." Hearing this, Tokusan just turned around and walked back to his quarters without a word. Can you imagine Tokusan's refinement and humility to allow his *tenzo* to speak to him like that and then just to turn around meekly and go back to his room? He was living without any pretension and far beyond any stink of Zen.

Seppo was really excited about this encounter and could hardly wait to tell his best buddy, Ganto. As soon as the meal was over, he ran over to Ganto and said, "Ganto, Ganto, guess what happened? I finally got the old man! He was heading down to the dining room too early so I shouted at him, 'Hey, old man, where the hell are you going?' and you know, with his tail between his legs, he just slunk back to his room!" Ganto, who was thirty-five at the time, replied, "Wow, you really did get him. Great master though he is, Tokusan has not yet grasped the last word of Zen!" Seppo must have wondered, "The last word of Zen? What is the last word of Zen?"

Later Tokusan heard what Ganto had said to Seppo and told his attendant, "Call Ganto to my room!" When Ganto entered, Tokusan said, "Word has gotten back to me that you don't approve of this old master." Ganto thereupon whispered in Tokusan's ear and, hearing what he said, Tokusan was satisfied and remained silent. The next day, Tokusan delivered a Dharma talk that was different from any he had ever given before. Ganto jumped up laughing and clapping his hands in the front of the meditation hall, exclaiming, "What a great joy it is! The old master has now grasped the last word of Zen. From now on nobody in the world can ever make light of him."

Now, if you presented this koan to your teacher in interview, he would ask you at least three questions: "What is the last word of Zen?" "What did Ganto whisper in Tokusan's ear that satisfied him?" and "What was different about Tokusan's talk that made Ganto jump up laughing and clapping?" You would need to satisfy the teacher with correct responses to these questions before he would pass you.

Can you see why I love Ganto? Though he is young and still immature, not even comparable to old Tokusan, what a scenario he sets up! What compassion, what skillful means! Even at thirty-five years old, Ganto's wisdom was enough to hook Seppo completely. For years Seppo had no choice but to ask, "What is the last word of Zen? What could it be?" That is what we call a natural koan, the heart of all koans, the basic question. You can imagine what Seppo's sitting was like for the next few years, working in the kitchen, never at peace.

A few years later Tokusan died. In search of a new teacher, Ganto and Seppo were on their way to see another great master. Still Seppo had not really attained true enlightenment. He had had some glimpses, but was not completely clear. One night while they were traveling, they stopped in an abandoned hut and laid out their blankets to sleep. In the middle of the night, Ganto awoke to see the candle still lit, the incense burning, and Seppo sitting in zazen. He said, "Hey, Seppo, what are you doing?" Seppo shouted back, "What does it look like I am doing?" Ganto replied, "What are you doing zazen for? Are you not going to sleep during the night?" Seppo declared, "To attain enlightenment, to realize Buddha!" Ganto responded, "Don't you realize, that which gushes out of your own heart *is* the Buddha?"

This story hits on the key point: that which gushes out of your own heart is nothing but the Buddhadharma, so what are you searching all over for? When you empty yourself of all opinions, notions, concepts, and ideas of self; when you become thoroughly void of ego; when you sit here as zero, as nothing; then what comes out of your heart is the true Dharma. And when one of my students gives a talk and expresses the true Dharma, I get even more excited than I was at the birth of my own baby. Even though I delivered her myself, it was not such a thrill as seeing someone overflowing with the Dharma. We say that the greatest miracle is the birth of a child, but to me that is second—the birth of a Buddha is far greater! Look how many babies are born, but how many Buddhas?

When you let go and stop clinging to your own opinions, ideas, and preferences, then you realize the one Truth, absolute reality, the One that can never change. When you are just sitting doing nothing, truly sitting, not seeking anything, not counting or following your breaths, not labeling, not working on a koan, but simply sitting there doing absolutely nothing, it seems really boring and difficult sometimes. You feel like you are getting nowhere, not accomplishing anything. In fact, you feel like you are just wasting your time; nothing exciting or new is happening.

You are just facing the Truth, which is always old. The Truth has been around a long time, a lot longer than Buddhism. It has always been; it always will be. There is only one Truth, but an infinite number of lies; so when we dwell in nonreality, when we live in the lies, it is exciting, like an action-packed adventure at the movies or on television. But the Truth is very old and rather boring. I would tell you what it is, but I forgot—it slipped my mind.

> *Those who do not live in the single Way*
> *fail in both activity and passivity,*
> *assertion and denial.*

He is talking about the way we live in lies, the way we go along with the social conspiracy: "Don't tell me the truth and I will not tell you the truth; don't tell me I am a fake and I will not tell you you are a fake." What is it that we are all concealing? Let's make it more intimate: what is it that *you* are concealing? What is it that you don't want anybody to find out? The same thing that everyone expends so much effort and energy to conceal: *that you don't know!* What is it that you don't know? Who you are, what you are! Once you can admit that, you can even live comfortably with not knowing.

Once Maezumi Roshi and I were riding on the bullet train in Japan. Roshi was sitting next to me and there was a couple opposite us. The husband was a board member at Zen Center of Los Angeles, visiting Japan at the same time Roshi and I were there. His wife was not involved in Zen. While we were talking, she looked over at Roshi and said, "You know, of all the men I have ever met, you are probably the most comfortable with not knowing who you are." Most of us are busy covering up, pretending to be something or somebody, often somebody important or special or intelligent or good, putting up some facade. When we sit, just letting thoughts arise and pass away, we begin to see: "Wait a minute, I did not realize that there was a gap between these thoughts. It never dawned on me that maybe I am not just these thoughts, I am not what I thought I was." At that point we begin to question. "What did I really think I was, anyway?"

We have constructed our own reality and put all our effort and energy into holding it together. We call that reality "life" or "sanity" and we take part in a social conspiracy, a common lie that we have all tacitly agreed to live by: "This is the way it is." We even believe that everybody else is living in the same world and sees things basically the same way we do. When somebody disagrees with our way of seeing, we are even capable of going to war and killing because their view is different from ours. We have fights between nations and even between different religious or ethnic groups in the name of defending shared lies.

Why do we hold on so tightly? Why do we make it a matter of life and death? Why is it we would rather suffer miserably than admit we might be wrong? Someone said to me in interview one day, "I realized something amazing: I got to that edge, I was just about to go over, and then I thought, 'Now, wait a minute, why am I leaping into the unknown? I don't want to; I want to keep my job!' I realized that this was the only thing keeping me from it: I am not ready to give up what I have, even though it may be false and a hell to live with—at least it is secure, safe, and familiar. It is like an uncomfortable old chair, but I am used to it. What lies ahead? I don't know!"

When I give up all that is familiar, when I let go, when I stop trying to understand, to figure everything out, I don't know what will happen. No one can know beforehand; it is impossible even to know what is going to happen the next minute or even the next second. To reach the truth, we must go through our fear. Fear is guarding the doorway to reality, fear of stepping off the hundred-foot pole, of letting go of who we think we are, of what we cherish, of our identity.

Whatever we identify with has to be dropped. Then what? "I'll be nobody, I'll be nothing!" That's right! We will become real, become what everybody is: a nothing, an empty vessel. Hold on to our identifications and we get nothing; let them go and we are filled up. But what do we usually do? We cling to our limited, petty existence for dear life. The feeling is that if we really let it go, we would lose everything. And what if we do lose it all? Is it so wonderful to be constricted, imprisoned? Is the jail cell of our lives really that comfortable? Have we really decorated it that nicely?

Somebody once told me, "I wish I had gotten into Zen practice earlier, before I took on all these responsibilities, before I had a wife, a job, and a mortgage." Of course, that is just avoiding the issue. There is absolutely nothing restricting us; it only appears so. The restriction is all in the mind. There are no restrictions, no barriers, no walls. When we realize what is most important, this great matter, the grave matter of life and death, then we also realize that nothing can prevent our accomplishing the Way. There is no distance too great, no ocean too vast, no mortgage too big, no spouse too demanding. All these "problems" are excuses to disguise the fact that really we just aren't ready to do it. It is scary to give everything up, to let it all go. Into what? For what? "Will I get something? Will I at last understand something? Will I gain something precious? Enlightenment? Sure, great! I'll be enlightened! I'll be a Buddha!" When you truly lose everything, you gain everything, which is absolutely nothing.

To deny the reality of things
is to miss their reality;
to assert the emptiness of things
is to miss their reality.

It is very simple. If we fall either into affirmation or into negation, we miss it. That's why whenever a monk came face to face with Tokusan, he would get hit no matter what he said. If we say a word, we affirm it; if we don't say a word, we negate it. If we both affirm and negate, we also miss it; but if we neither affirm nor negate, we still miss it. There is no way out. This koan, Tokusan's Thirty Blows, is called the Killing Sword of Tokusan. There is no winning in this one! If you think you can win, you lose; but when you truly lose, you win.

When you come to the end of the line, no place left to run or hide, and you can't find an answer or even a comfortable place to rest anywhere, when you are completely desperate, disillusioned, bewildered, then at that point you recognize you are so close, so very close! You think, "At the very bottom it could not be any worse. I don't understand a thing. I have been sitting now for fifteen years and I know less than ever. I don't know what has happened; I don't know where I am going; I don't know what all this is about; I don't even know any longer who I am or why I am here or why I am doing this."

Congratulations! Then it takes only one more tiny little step and you are off the hundred-foot pole. Leap! Don't back away, don't run from it. When you give it all up, you get it all. You end up losing absolutely nothing, other than some well cherished opinions and ideas.

Why do we fear, why do we resist so much letting people close to us go through what they must go through and face what they must face? We say we love them, but can it be love if we are trying to stop them from realizing themselves? After all, we aren't likely to lose our spouse if we have a sound marriage in the first place, and we stand to gain an awakened human being, a Buddha. Certainly we may be afraid of losing the relationship along the way, but even more we may fear having to feel our own pain watching them go through their anguish—and how we dread having to go through the pain of change ourselves! True compassion means having the trust to remain completely open in every situation and the confidence to respond freely without fear of hurting yourself or others.

Over and over again, I would come to Maezumi Roshi and say, "So-and-so is in such pain, what can we do?" He would reply, "Let him suffer! Let him go through it!" And I thought, "How cruel!" Yet what is a Bodhisattva but someone who allows others to go through what they must go through? Everybody else is trying to stop the pain, patching him up and patting him on the back and saying, "It's OK, dear, everything is going to be all right." Everybody is conspiring to cover things up.

When you rob a person of his pain and suffering, you rob him of his life, his freedom, his independence; you keep him dependent on you. This is a trap for therapists and healers and Zen teachers, too. After all, where would any of us be without our patients and students? But our practice is to get ourselves standing on our own two feet as quickly as possible and then to help others do the same. Ironically, it is the ones we most cherish whom we most often rob of their independence, because we tend to shield and overprotect them.

> *The more you talk and think about it,*
> *the further astray you wander from the truth.*

Trying to grasp it by thinking is like trying to contain the whole ocean in a single cup. Thinking is so limited, while the One Mind is vast and wide like infinite space. There is no way that thoughts or words can touch it. All we can do is sit quietly, stop looking outside ourselves and turn inward, dropping our cherished opinions about reality, about ourselves, about our own importance. When we sit, we begin to see our huge ego everywhere. We start to realize how greedy and self-centered we are.

> *Stop talking and thinking*
> *and there is nothing you will not be able to know.*

Dwell in not-knowing, abide in that open space. When you don't know anything, you know *everything*. Are you worried about how you are going to handle tomorrow? What you are going to do? Don't know! Tomorrow will take care of itself. Just be completely present and attentive now, here, and don't know. Then you will respond appropriately to whatever situation comes up. You don't need rules and regulations to do that. All you need is to have faith in yourself. If you cling to rules, you just bind and restrict yourself and destroy your freedom. If you want to be free, let go of all that is binding you, every should and shouldn't, do and don't; "I can't do that, I must not do that, I shouldn't do that, I don't dare do that."

> *To return to the root is to find the meaning,*
> *but to pursue appearances is to miss the source.*

When we turn the mind inward, that is called "returning to the root." Find your source, the very root of your own existence. Look in, don't think about it or try to figure it out, just turn your own light inward and penetrate to the very core, to the very bottom, to the very essence of your being. Be intimate with that source, at one, then you will dwell in not-knowing. At that point, nothing is known; anything known already becomes two, already a duality. With that one Truth, there is no division between knower and known, subject and object; there is just the One, your true nature, your real self.

> *At the moment of inner enlightenment,*
> *there is a going beyond appearance and emptiness.*
> *The changes that appear to occur in the empty world*
> *we call real only because of our ignorance.*

All the changes, the coming and going, that we think are so real—all our heartbreaks and upsets and emotions—we only call real because of our ignorance, because we don't see the true reality. We are stuck in appearances.

> *Do not search for the truth;*
> *only cease to cherish opinions.*

How can he be saying not to look for truth? Because if you seek after *anything*, even truth, you have already gone astray. The moment you begin seeking, you have left your own home, you have left the seat of the Buddha. When you sit on your meditation cushion, you are sitting on the seat of the Buddha, the seat of the Awakened One. You *are* the Truth. Christ said it: "I am the Way," but he was misunderstood. You *are* the Way. *You* are the Truth, the Dharma, the Buddha. Don't search for it outside yourself.

On New Year's Day it was traditional at Zen Center of Los Angeles for us to visit the grave of Senzaki Sensei, the first Japanese Zen teacher to settle in America. He came over with Soyen Shaku Roshi and D. T. Suzuki around 1891 and was the first teacher of Aitken Roshi. On his gravestone is written an ancient saying of the Buddha that expresses this truth beautifully: "Do not put another head above your own."

Every moment of every single day you are manifesting the true reality, only you don't realize it. We practice to realize it, but we also practice because that is our Way. That is the reality and that is the realization. When you take the posture of zazen, your true nature is in realization. When you just sit there, not clinging to your opinions, not holding on to what is coming and going, you are in complete realization.

For many years Mullah Nasrudin used to cross the border frequently from Turkey to Hungary with only a donkey and a pack on its back filled with hay. The border guards were sure he was smuggling something, but they did not know what. Each time they would search more and more thoroughly. They would go through all the hay, even look in the donkey's mouth, but they never found anything.

One day one of the old border guards, who had by now retired, walked into a bar and there was Mullah drinking and having a good time, so he decided to find out the answer to the mystery. He went up to Nasrudin and said, "For fifteen years you have had us bewildered. We know you have been smuggling. Now listen, I am no longer on the border patrol. I give you my word of honor that I will not turn you in, but for my peace of mind, you must tell me: what in the world were you smuggling?" "Donkeys!" Mullah replied.

The Truth is the most obvious thing, yet we are always looking for a needle in a haystack. When you see the Truth, nothing changes. A tree is still a tree, a mountain is a mountain. As Maezumi Roshi once said, "I can't believe all the suffering and frustration people go through only to realize that a table is a table, a chair is a chair."

4 *Undisturbed in the Way*

Do not remain in the dualistic state;
avoid such pursuits carefully.
If there is even a trace
of this and that, of right and wrong,
the Mind-essence will be lost in confusion.
Although all dualities come from the One,
do not be attached even to this One.
When the mind exists undisturbed in the Way,
nothing in the world can offend,
and when a thing can no longer offend,
it ceases to exist in the old way.

Do not remain in the dualistic state;
avoid such pursuits carefully.

The key point here is to cease seeing things in a dualistic way,
to free ourselves from dualistic ideas and ultimately from dualistic consciousness itself. This process begins with sitting. If we
are constantly judging our sitting, "Oh, this is terrible sitting,"
or "I am not sitting as well as I was last period or last retreat,"
or "I should not be thinking these kinds of thoughts, having these
fantasies or feelings," or "I should not be thinking at all," right
there we are caught in the dualistic state. Our zazen is to practice
nonthinking and if we sit there scolding ourselves, that is certainly not practicing nonthinking. When we simply allow the
mind's natural function to take place, then thoughts will arise,
just as bubbles rise to the surface of water. That is the natural
function of the mind, just as the natural function of the ocean is
to have waves.

If we can leave them alone, not giving them any special importance by loving them or hating them, clinging to them or rejecting them, and simply allow ourselves to be empty space, infinite space, where any thoughts at all may come and go, then they will simply dissolve of their own accord. Just as waves come and go, rising and falling, just as bubbles come to the surface and burst, so thoughts will appear and disappear.

Our mind in its natural state is like a mirror, simply reflecting what comes before it. What appears in the mind is not separate from it. Mind and objects are not two. All things are nothing but Mind; but this Mind is not the small egoistic mind, very limited in its perspective and capacity, with which we normally identify.

How have we become trapped in this narrow little mind? Knowingly or unknowingly, we have built up over many years a fixed position made up of beliefs and habits. We have been taught from early childhood onward how to act in every situation and what views to hold. When we walk into a shop, when we go to an art gallery or attend a film or a play, we are expected to have opinions about everything. And every time we meet other people, we are expected to form judgments about them. Our lives are made up almost entirely of unconscious attitudes and habits that govern everything we do, from brushing our teeth to interacting with others.

When we sit in ritual situations, such as meditation retreats, it is easier for us to see unconscious habitual patterns of thought and action. If we have a structure with certain rules and regulations that helps us to slow down and face ourselves, then it becomes harder to avoid noticing the numerous ways we think and feel and act automatically.

Once when I was at an insight meditation retreat, we were asked to take five precepts during our stay. One of them was not to take anything that isn't yours or given to you. I happened to have forgotten my toothpaste, so I brushed for two or three days without any. Then I noticed a roommate's tube of toothpaste sitting out on the counter. I thought, "Using a little bit of his toothpaste is not going to bother him. I'm sure if he were here, he would give it to me." I had nearly finished squeezing it out on the brush before I realized that I was breaking the vow I had taken.

Ordinarily in life situations like this, we say to ourselves, "So what? Nobody is watching me and nobody really cares about it. What difference does it make?" But aren't our vast social problems the sum total of countless "so whats"? "So what if I cheat and steal!" "So what if I rape and kill!" Where do we draw the line between a "so what" that is too minor to worry about and another that is big enough to matter?

Our practice is to become aware and attentive, to wake up. It is not enough to be aware only when we sit zazen, we must become attentive throughout our lives, twenty-four hours a day. If awakened mind does not carry over into our lives, then who are we kidding? What are we doing sitting, then? Just putting ourselves through a masochistic ordeal of leg pain? We are here to awaken, to attain panoramic awareness, *anuttara samyak sambodhi*, the supreme awakening, ultimate wisdom.

Often awareness begins by our noticing what we are doing right after we do it. That is a start—at least we are noticing it then. When we are in the midst of an argument with our boyfriend or girlfriend, husband or wife, we don't realize what is happening, how caught up we are in our own position. That same evening we may sit down to do zazen and the incident plays back in our minds. Then we ask ourselves, "What was I fighting about? Why was I so determined to be right? Why did I cause such a problem, such misery for both of us?" If we are not awake enough to notice and step back at the moment it is happening, at least we notice when we sit on our cushion. Of course, if we never sit down, we may go on being unconscious indefinitely and never notice it.

As we become more and more attentive, more alert, we will become aware the moment the fight is over. We will no longer have to wait until we sit down on the cushion to realize, "I was being self-centered. I was really holding on to my position. I will go and apologize." Maybe we just told someone the truth, but in a very inappropriate way. We notice that we could have said it more tactfully, in such a way that the person did not need to get defensive.

My teacher always made this point: the way we say things makes all the difference in the world—whether with a compassionate heart or insensitively, out of our egoistic mind. We are being tested on this point twenty-four hours a day and we wonder why our relationships don't work. No matter how many communication workshops we have attended, if there is communication without awareness and sensitivity, it is not much help to others. The essential issue is how sensitive and aware we are in our everyday life. That is what it means to be a Buddha: to be awake twenty-four hours a day, even while sleeping.

An awakened one is not a person who merely has had some kind of experience and then goes on to live his or her life unconsciously, insensitively, inattentively. If you see someone on the street having difficulty while you are out walking and you take the time to stop, go over to them, and see what the problem is, that is being aware, that is responding to the situation. When you are all involved with your own thoughts and problems, caught up in your own emotions, you might not even notice that another person is in need.

Our practice is not to be self-absorbed. Our practice is not to sit on the cushion only to become lost in our own thoughts and feelings. Certainly we have to experience thoughts and emotions. We certainly ought not to block them out of our awareness, but we need not get caught up in them. Our practice is to clear the space for these thoughts and feelings to arise and then to disperse, dissolve, disappear of their own accord. When they arise, there is just attention, just awareness without judgment, without saying, "This thought is rotten," or, "This one is great; I must remember it."

> *If there is even a trace*
> *of this and that, of right and wrong,*
> *the Mind-essence will be lost in confusion.*

If there is even the thought that he or she is not me, if there is even the idea that the tree and I are separate, then dualistic thinking arises and confusion happens. When you are sitting in *shikantaza*, allow the mind and heart to include everything. Do not exclude anything or anybody. Include all that arises. When you are sitting, don't concentrate on one thing and exclude other things, just hold the mind awake, alert, and attentive. You can concentrate on simply allowing everything to happen. Concentrate on holding your mind and your posture open. You can concentrate on resting the mind in the palm of your left hand, neither creating artificial barriers nor excluding anything. Just hold the mind alert and attentive but not abiding any place in particular, just allowing things to settle. The more you can hold your body still, the more the mind has the opportunity to settle down.

> *Although all dualities come from the One,*
> *do not be attached even to this One.*

Everything arises from the One, the One Mind. Trees, mountains, blue sky, clouds, all thoughts and emotions, don't attach to any of it and don't attach to the experience of Oneness either. Just remain unattached to everything that arises, holding no preferences.

> *When the mind exists undisturbed in the Way,*
> *nothing in the world can offend,*
> *and when a thing can no longer offend,*
> *it ceases to exist in the old way.*

Think about how easily we become disturbed or offended when somebody corrects our posture or tells us we are doing something improperly. In meditation retreats we have an opportunity to observe our minds, our behavior, our ways of relating to the world. We have a chance to see how easily we resist or get angry. How we deal with that anger or resistance makes all the difference in the world, whether we just notice it and then immediately drop it or get caught up in it for a few days or longer. If we hold on to it, there is one person who is definitely going to suffer, and maybe many more.

One day I was talking with my mother in a restaurant, discussing religious people. My grandmother hated them all—priests, rabbis, all kinds of religious persons. My grandmother's father had been a rabbi who loved to meditate, pray, study the Torah, and teach. But as he did not like to spend time with his family, she felt neglected. As a result, all her life she has despised religious people, though she does not recognize the cause. (Thank God she does not consider me a religious person!) I said to my mother, "What about just forgiving your grandfather? You have been carrying around your mother's hatred for so long!" "I could not possibly do that," she answered. "But who is suffering?" I asked. "Is he suffering because of it? Are you making him miserable? Are you getting even? He has been dead for seventy or eighty years!"

We don't think clearly. We hold on to our hatred and resentment, not realizing that the one we are really hurting is ourself. When we can just let go and forgive the other, the one we are helping is ourself. And what is this practice if it is not to let go, to surrender? What is true zazen but that very process of being open, that process of continuously letting go and surrendering every moment? But surrendering to what? It really does not matter what we call it: God or the Tao or the Dharma or the Buddha or our true nature. They are all concepts anyway. It is the act of letting go, of surrendering, that matters. The very act of letting go opens us up completely.

What does it take to surrender? Trust. Faith. We must have the faith that when we let go we will not really go insane or die. We are only just dropping body and mind, but just before it happens it feels like going insane. And it is true: we are going out of our minds! That is the whole point: to let ourselves go beyond the mind, to stop dwelling in the mind. The problem with Western society is that we live in our heads—that is why we are creating such a mess! Dogs and cats and trees don't dwell in their heads. Trees and animals do not create such chaos.

Who is upsetting the whole balance of nature? Who is destroying the ozone layer? Who is wiping out all the forests? Who could destroy the whole planet? Who but us, through the very technology our tremendous mental ability has produced. There is nothing wrong with having great mental capacity, but in our case it is like giving a very sharp knife to a young child. We don't have the maturity to use our minds properly yet.

Our educational system is completely unbalanced. I taught in it for eight years and experienced this firsthand. We teach only to the head, with maybe twenty minutes a day for the body, but nothing for the whole person. In order to do a little meditation exercise in a public school I had to call it "concentration," and only then was it permitted. If I called it "meditation" it would be associated with religion and, of course, you can't teach religion in American public schools. Zazen goes far beyond religion, but not many people realize that.

When we were in Japan and went to see the *zenji*, the equivalent of the pope in the Soto Zen hierarchy, he asked in Japanese, "Can any of the non-Japanese here understand our language?" The Japanese people present assured him that we could not. Then he stated in Japanese, "Western minds can never grasp the true *shobo* [the true Dharma], they are too objective." He meant that we see ourselves as subject and everything else as an object.

He was right. Western civilization is responsible for polluting our environment and could easily destroy the planet, fundamentally as a result of this dualistic way of perceiving. The Eastern mind tends to be much more in harmony with nature. It sees nature more as a whole, not as something separate and apart from the mind that tries constantly to conquer and dominate nature. The Native Americans are the same in this respect, much more in tune with nature, with the Way. In our Western society we have gotten completely out of tune with the natural order of things. Of course, in recent times the East has been absorbing and imitating this unbalanced Western mind.

The *zenji* was saying that the Western mind is just too stuck in the objective way of perceiving ever to grasp the true Dharma. Since one of the Americans there spoke Japanese quite fluently, I learned what the *zenji* had said. That evening we met with some other high Soto officials who were right under the *zenji* in the hierarchy, all of them roshis over fifty years old. They had the opportunity to ask us questions, but since they did not really want to do so, I spoke up: "This afternoon when we met with the *zenji*, he said that the Western mind could never grasp the true *shobo*, the true essence of Dogen Zenji." Then, in my green and immature way, I added, "I have to agree with the *zenji* that probably we cannot grasp the true *shobo*, but what about the Japanese mind? Can *it* grasp the true *shobo*?"

Arrogant as it must have sounded, it was a valid question. First of all, can the true *shobo* be grasped, whether by an Eastern or a Western mind? Can the mind grasp the Mind? Or, to put it experientially, can we really live twenty-four hours a day following Dogen Zenji's teaching? Hardly anyone lived up to his standards. He approved only a handful of Patriarchs prior to him. I doubt very much he would approve any of us walking the planet today.

Recently I had to make a bow to the *zenji* in appreciation. He is really a true master. He hooked me. Now I am absolutely determined that we manifest the true *shobo* in the West, if it is the last thing we do! The teaching will not die, and that old man made sure of it.

5 Objects Vanish, Mind Vanishes

When no discriminating thoughts arise,
the old mind ceases to exist.
When thought objects vanish,
the thinking-subject vanishes,
as when the mind vanishes, objects vanish.
Things are objects because there is a subject or mind;
and the mind is a subject because there are objects.
Understand the relativity of these two
and the basic reality: the unity of emptiness.
In this Emptiness the two are indistinguishable
and each contains in itself the whole world.
If you do not discriminate between coarse and fine
you will not be tempted to prejudice and opinion.

When no discriminating thoughts arise,
the old mind ceases to exist.

In the absence of discriminating thoughts, the mind as we
know it ceases to exist. Our suffering—our feeling of discomfort,
alienation, loneliness—arises because we create a dualistic way
of perceiving everything that separates us from the external.
When we view the so-called external phenomenal world as
distinct from ourselves, then fear arises, fear that we will lose
our lives, that we may not continue to exist. Out of that fear
come anger, jealousy, greed, hatred, aversion, attachment—all
kinds of clinging. All our problems arise out of seeing ourselves

as separate entities. We cling to what we perceive as *me*: *my* physical body and *my* ideas, *my* mind, *my* thoughts, *my* understanding, *my* beliefs, *my* concepts, *my* opinions.

The Third Patriarch is telling us to stop cherishing our own opinions and clinging to our personal preferences. When we stop holding on to our likes and dislikes, our attachment and aversion toward everything and everyone, then the mind as we now know it ceases to exist. This is what is called dropping the mind or forgetting the self. When we forget the self, then any object in the external world ceases to exist in the familiar way, as a separate object outside ourselves. Then all objects are no other than ourselves: the mountains, the trees, the rocks, the grasses, the blue sky, the moon, everything—all One Mind, Buddha Mind. Everything in existence, all that arises, not only material objects but also thoughts and emotions, is nothing but Mind, nothing but the Buddhadharma. We can call it God or the source or one's true nature. Whatever name we give it, it is all One, One Mind. Joshu, the famous Chinese Zen master, called it *mu*. When asked by a monk, "Does a dog have Buddha-nature?" Joshu answered, "*Mu!*" The koan, "What is *mu*?" gives the Zen student the opportunity to realize the One Mind directly.

Once that inner transformation has taken place, all attachment drops away. Clinging and aversion both disappear. Aversion is really just another form of clinging. If I don't like what you are, it is because I am attached to a different picture of how I want you to be. My aversion to you is just the opposite side of my attachment to the ideal picture of you that I am holding in my mind. This is the cause of most of our relationship problems, holding on to our pictures of how we want our wife, husband, children, parents to be. Because of the pictures that we cherish, these people can never live up to our expectations. If they did, then they would not be true to themselves. They would be living a lie by trying to fit themselves into our pictures.

What then can we do? Must we continue trying to change everyone? Or could we do what is simplest and most direct: drop our preconceived notions, our pictures and concepts of how others should be? Then we could allow others the space to be just what they are. And when we really accept others exactly as they are, tremendous faith and trust arise. Meeting someone who has that much faith in us allows us to believe in ourselves, to accept at the deepest level that we are OK. And if we are not OK, that is all right, too. I have all kinds of hang-ups. I have attachments and aversions, quirks and idiosyncrasies. So what! We all do. The more we accept and trust ourselves, the more we see that *it*—Buddha-nature, true self, source, God, master, enlightenment, call it what you will—is *me*!

The other side of the coin is that I am not *it*. What we normally define as who we are, this particular body and mind, is not *it*. The light, the divine, Buddha-nature, no matter what we call it, only comes *through* me, as it comes through you. When we drop attachment to body and mind there is no distinction between *it* and self. As the Third Patriarch says, any distinction we make sets heaven and earth infinitely apart. If we attach to the notion that "I am *it*," then our egos swell up and we become very arrogant. We must avoid clinging to the experience of enlightenment, the realization of being *it*. It flows through me; I am just a conduit.

What is all this stuff we call self? Just our own opinions, ideas, beliefs, concepts, likes, and dislikes: I like her, I hate him; I want this, I don't want that. All these distinctions show concern only for my own good. When we cease to cherish such opinions, this is called emptying the cup. And it is not enough just to empty the cup: we have to break out the very bottom! Why? So that the Dharma can flow through. It is not enough just to receive the teaching, to fill ourselves with more distinctions labeled Dharma. We must be totally open, bottomless. How? By constantly sitting and continuously ceasing to cherish opinions for and against anything. When we stop holding on to our preferences, our lives go very smoothly and harmoniously, for then we are in accord with the Dharma.

> *When thought objects vanish,*
> *the thinking-subject vanishes,*
> *as when the mind vanishes, objects vanish.*

When we look into the mind with the mind, we are focusing the light inward that is normally being diffused externally. We see a beautiful woman or man and right away we are distracted from simply experiencing that. Coveting and craving enter: we dream of possessing him or her, holding on to the object of our desire. Our minds react that way when we are titillated by any of the six senses: seeing, hearing, smelling, tasting, feeling, and thinking.

If we have a wonderful thought, we cherish it and cling to it; but if we have a terrible thought, such as hating or killing, we detest ourselves for that. If we see something ugly, smell something stinky, right away we reject it. Why can't we just hear, just see, just have thoughts, just feel; just work, just sit, just listen, without adding our judgments—wouldn't that be a lot easier?

Things are objects because there is a subject or mind;
and the mind is a subject because there are objects.

In other words, subject and object are in relationship; one cannot exist without the other. There is no subject without objects as references, no self without something other than self. Therefore, if I really want to exist, I have to create you out there separate from me as something I can possess, like my wife or son or daughter or student. Self and object reinforce each other. Drop one and the other disappears. It doesn't matter which we drop. Drop the self and objects disappear. Cease to focus on objects and the self disappears. Body and mind drop.

All dualities work like this. Life and death together are a duality. The moment you are born, you are going to die. Thus death is created the moment life comes into being. If someone is not born they will never die. Life and death are inseparable, just one continuum. Life contains death and death includes life. When you die, already rebirth is on the way. And yet life is life and death is death. So when we are living, why not just live, and when we die, just die? While we are alive why worry about dying? If we have some old worn-out clothes we throw them away—why cling to them? When it is time for this body to become dust, just let it go.

The greatest gift anyone can be given is freedom from fear. That is what we practice for: to let go of all fear with the clarity that we call *prajna*, to look deeply into the matter of life and death. Let go of fear of dying, fear of living, fear of doing, and fear of not doing. We are afraid to do and afraid not to do, afraid just to sit and equally afraid to act, to throw ourselves wholeheartedly into our lives.

Why are we so afraid? If you put yourself totally into any activity, you disappear in that activity, you dissolve. Then there is no self. Our usual existence is like a semicoma, a paralysis; we are too scared really to live and too frightened to die. When we drop the fear of dying, we are no longer afraid to live, either, and we can live fully at last. And when it comes time to die, then that is just another part of living also. We can totally let go and die wholeheartedly. True living is letting go of body and mind every moment; allowing all things to exist just as they are; releasing everything, no longer being attached to any preferences.

> *Understand the relativity of these two*
> *and the basic reality: the unity of emptiness.*
> *In this Emptiness the two are indistinguishable*
> *and each contains in itself the whole world.*

Life contains everything. Death contains everything. Each thing contains everything. If we focus on self, the whole world is nothing but self. If our attention is on the other, then the whole world is nothing but that other. If we feel good, it is all good; if bad, then it is all bad.

What more wonderful, glorious, miraculous, splendid thing can there be than this world? Every winter the trees go dormant—it is almost like death. Then spring comes, and everything comes back to life. Flowers bloom, leaves unfurl. Then summer arrives—it is glorious! After that fall comes with its vivid colors and tremendous beauty, then winter again, over and over. Every day the sun comes up, giving light for us to see and to make distinctions in color and form. Then daylight fades and the darkness of night follows, making things almost indistinguishable until dawn comes again.

Of course, we can choose to feel that everything is awful. Every day is a bad day and we are always suffering. Why do we suffer? Nothing ever goes the way we want it to go: we want more or we want something else; we want ourselves to be different or others to be different. We are losing our bodies; they are growing old, decaying, falling apart, and everything looks grim, terrible. If we feel it is bad, everything becomes bad; if we feel it is good, then it all appears good.

The whole world is created from Mind. How we perceive it is the whole story. If we see everything from our ego-centered view, everything is too much to handle. Always we feel limited, unable to cope with situations. We feel small, helpless, and out of control. If we go beyond the egoistic view of the self as separate, then we can enjoy a more magnanimous, panoramic perspective that we can call Limitless Mind (*dai shin*), infinite capacity and complete faith in things just the way they are. It all depends on how we choose to view life. Dropping the ego-centered self we discover the real self, which is none other than no fixed self, completely open to each moment of life.

> *If you do not discriminate between coarse and fine*
> *you will not be tempted to prejudice and opinion.*

But discriminating is just what we are doing all the time: "I don't like this junk food, I eat only natural food," or "This is polyester, I wear only cotton." In fact, we even pride ourselves on our distinctions. We say that middle-class America wears polyester and eats junk like hamburgers, french fries, hot dogs. We wear cotton and eat whole foods. They promote war and nuclear power and kill whales. We are for a beautiful and safe environment. We are good and they are bad. We are clever and they are stupid. We are righteous and they are not.

Why do we make such distinctions and cling to them? It appears to make us feel good about ourselves, to feel important and right, but does it really work? Can we really feel good about ourselves when we are hating and despising? We talk about love, but what do we mean by it? To love only certain people, the ones who don't wear polyester? Can we drop all our opinions for and against everything? That is what the Third Patriarch is asking of us.

Resistance to this idea immediately comes up, resistance in the form of conflict, a head full of thoughts and fears, and lack of trust. The basic fear is, "Who would I be without my opinions and notions?" That's the point! *You* wouldn't be. You would cease to exist in the old way. Who, then, would you be? Buddha. *Mu.* Now every moment is fresh; every moment you are new. In the midst of coming and going, there is no coming and going. In the midst of being born and dying, you cease to be born and to die. How? Don't ask how! Just do. Just sit. Let go of body and mind. Forget yourself.

6 Neither Coming nor Going

To live in the Great Way
is neither easy nor difficult.
But those with limited views
are fearful and irresolute:
the faster they hurry, the slower they go.
Clinging cannot be limited;
even to be attached to the idea of enlightenment
is to go astray.
Just let things be in their own way
and there will be neither coming nor going.

To live in the Great Way
is neither easy nor difficult.

To live in the Great Way is to live without limits or boundaries. It is not a matter of being easy or difficult. It is simply the Way. Just allow everything to be as it is. It is so simple, but we always create unnecessary complications. On top of what is we put our preferences and aversions. We won't simply see things and accept them as they are. A primary benefit of practice is to remove the colored lenses that distort our view of reality or Dharma or truth. When we sit and practice with great determination, we actually experience the disappearance of these lenses that have come between ourselves and everything else.

What enables us to practice with such determination? The bottom line is faith, trust. If we don't trust, we simply cannot practice. How do you know if you have enough trust? If you sit regularly as much as possible and attend retreats when you can, that shows your faith. We all find reasons not to sit, excuses that seem genuine and valid, but that frequently arise from our resistance to sitting and facing ourselves, facing our lives. Sitting through resistance, staying with it through the rough times, requires immense faith.

This is what practice is: to study the self, to realize the self, and thereby to actualize the self. When? All the time. How? By being ourselves, not by being somebody different, someone else's picture of how we should be. We can never live up to another's picture of who and how we ought to be, so we feel bad about ourselves, guilty. We become tense and we create tension for others.

Sometimes we have very strange ideas about practice in relation to accomplishing the Way. For example, more than twenty-two years ago I studied karate intensively for just over a year. Then three years ago I took up karate again after twenty years of little or no training. I consider myself still a beginner and would never claim to be an accomplished or senior karate student just because I started my training many years back. Sometimes in our Zen training, just because we have been practicing for fifteen or twenty years doing occasional retreats and a little sitting each day, we get the notion that we should be considered senior or accomplished Zen students. The number of years since we started to sit is not very important. What really counts is the intensity of our practice and the depth of our realization.

What is true realization? "I am *it*. I am the Way." That is what we all realize when we sit and practice intently: "I am the Truth. I am the Dharma. I am the Buddha." This is the first true opening, to be able at last to admit this. Up until that point, we can hear it over and over again, but we can't digest it, we can't even swallow it. Somehow we feel so bad about ourselves, we have such a lack of faith in ourselves, that we can't really take it in. We think that Buddha is somebody else, that the master is someone other than ourselves.

That first opening, what we call *kensho,* is seeing into our nature and being able to affirm, "I am *it*." There is no separation from the whole: This is *it*. The experience is completely different from some concept in our heads about what Buddha is or what *mu* is. This very body and mind is *mu*! As soon as we pass through this transformation, we begin to take responsibility for ourselves. Up until this point we can blame others. We say God, the world, parents, husband, wife, children, boss, anybody and everybody else is at fault for the way our lives are. The truth is that nobody does anything to us. Realizing this, we become fully responsible in all situations and accept our lives as *this*. Then we are the master.

Buddha means the Awakened One. To awaken to our true nature is to be the Buddha. What does this mean? What do you realize through all this searching, seeking, effort, and determination? What do you discover? Absolutely nothing! We all seek to attain something, only to find that from the very beginning there was nothing to attain.

There is one koan where a Buddha sat for ten thousand aeons and never attained the Dharma. A Buddha practicing for so very long and not enlightened? Why? Because he is a nonattained Buddha. How can an awakened person awaken? This dreaming deluded state, this ignorant state we are in, is the awakened state! There is no other state, no other shore, and nothing else to be realized.

Then for what is all this struggling and seeking? Where are we trying to go? We cannot separate delusion and enlightenment, ignorance and realization, samsara and nirvana. This samsaric world is *it*! The problem is we don't accept that. We hold on to preferences and that is the cause of our suffering. So just put an end to conceptual thinking! How? Zazen! Practicing what? Nonthinking. What is nonthinking? Just sit and don't think. How do you sit and not think? Don't make any effort to think.

It is natural to have thoughts, but thinking requires effort. In the most natural state, there is nonthinking. What do we mean by nonthinking? Simply allowing thoughts to bubble up into the mind and pass away is nonthinking. Nonthinking is that which goes beyond either thoughts or no thoughts: it is neither blank mind nor busy mind. When the mind is allowed to rest naturally, there is no problem. We create a problem only if we don't like the thoughts that arise spontaneously and want to get rid of them. Then our thoughts persist all the more.

> *But those with limited views*
> *are fearful and irresolute:*
> *the faster they hurry, the slower they go.*

The perfect Way knows no difficulty. This Way is not a matter of difficult or easy, so just let it be! Those with limited views are fearful of realizing this. What do we mean by limited views? Think about it. We think one thing is good, another is bad; this is right, that is wrong. "Now, hitting someone, that is bad!" But what is wrong with hitting someone? Some of you have been hit when you came to *daisan*. Maybe it was the best thing—perhaps it woke you up. There is no absolute right or wrong. My karate teacher used to say that if you really want to know the truth about someone, hit them. Everybody can be nice if you are nice, loving if you are loving; but how do they behave if you hit them or give them a hard time?

If I say killing is not bad, the mind hears killing is good. Our minds always work either/or: if it is not this, then it must be that. If I say the ceiling is not high, then you hear me saying the ceiling is low, when simply the ceiling is neither particularly high nor especially low. Our minds create these polarities constantly.

Even such a basic thing as love is utterly misunderstood by our minds, all confused with self-clinging and attachment to objects. In Zen training, the hardest thing to take is not being treated as an object. Isn't that amazing? We would think no one would want to be treated as an object. Isn't that one of the issues in the women's movement, women not wanting to be treated as sexual objects by men? But look what happens when someone stops treating us as an object: "Don't I exist in your mind? Aren't I important? Aren't I somebody?" Isn't that our great fear—to lose our individuality, our selves? No longer to know who we are? In unconditional loving, we no longer have personality; we no longer have identity. In that moment, when we become One, subject and object disappear: we lose ourselves utterly.

When you come into *daisan* and are really open and vulnerable, then there is only love. That can be scary, because in this state of love there is no self. Feeling that you are losing yourself, the first thing you do is grab hold of your familiar identity. Fear comes up in your eyes: you are afraid to lose yourself and you tighten up. Then communion is finished. I may sit and chat with you, but the real encounter is over because you have closed down.

It is said that the teacher is a mirror. When you enter, the teacher is just there, with no preconceived notions or ideas. If you are too afraid just to be there also, without a self, with no boundary between you and the teacher, and you close up in fear, then the teacher reflects that right back so you can see exactly where you stand.

When two people are together without boundary, there is no object, so the subject also disappears; and vice versa, with no subject, the object disappears. That is called One Mind. That is true transmission. If we can say interview has a goal, it is two minds becoming one. Student becomes master, master becomes student—inseparable!

That is what practice is all about: you are to become the master. When you open yourself up, when you open your heart, when you are bottomless, empty, then the Dharma just flows. As long as you are holding on to likes and dislikes, opinions, prejudices, preferences, self-consciousness, it cannot happen. Not only do we have to empty the self of the self and be bottomless, we even have to wipe off whatever is sticking to the edges. Any residue of self remaining somehow discolors the flow. We have to wipe ourselves absolutely clean.

That is actually the meaning of *samu*, the work period: to wipe clean. We do not mean just wiping the carpet and the furniture clean, but also wiping mind and self clean. What is all this dirt and dust we must clean up? Delusions, defilements—all our opinions and views, *me* and *mine*. Holding on to our own personal perspectives, we remain confined and narrow, limited and small, suffering. Putting others before ourselves and doing for the sake of the Buddhadharma, we actualize limitless Mind.

When Maezumi Roshi left Japan as a twenty-four-year-old

monk, he made a vow to himself always to think of others first, never himself. It is an amazing vow, isn't it? It is not easy. Maybe it is too much. That vow caused him a lot of pain and suffering. But he accomplished much through all that pain and suffering. He gave interviews constantly. We used to beg him to take even just one day off or take time to sit, but he would not do it. He used to sit for five minutes, at most ten, then he would go straight into the *dokusan* room, because there would often be a hundred people to see. And he would stay two-and-a-half to three hours, four times a day. It was hard to keep up with him. I used to come home exhausted.

When I asked my karate teacher, whom I respect very much, "How have you managed to be so successful?," do you know what he told me? "I never think of myself, only what is good for people and good for the *dojo*." It was true. He was there every morning at four-thirty—I checked. I decided I would make that my practice and be there at four-thirty.

But what do we usually do? "I am too tired, too busy. It is too much for me." We get caught up in ourselves, in our emotions, in our thinking. Everything is too much. Let go of the self, forget the self, and nothing is too great. Consider what is good for the sake of the Buddhadharma and then do it; that always works. When we forget this, things may not work out so well.

> *Clinging cannot be limited;*
> *even to be attached to the idea of enlightenment*
> *is to go astray.*

Attachment to anything leads us astray, and especially attachment to enlightenment. For then enlightenment itself becomes our biggest obstacle, the ultimate delusion. Does that mean we should not have enlightenment? No. It means get enlightened and then drop it. Some of you might try to do what I tried to do, which was to drop enlightenment before I attained it, knowing a big attachment would arise. You should try first with all your might and main to realize enlightenment. Then when you finally realize it, just let go of it. How tricky this becomes, for when you realize what enlightenment is, you realize absolutely nothing;

and how can you get attached to nothing? But like magicians, we find a way to do it somehow.

It is like the story of Enyadatta, a woman who arose bleary-eyed one morning after a very hard night. She glanced into her mirror to admire herself, as she so often did, since she was quite vain and self-involved. The night before, her children had decided to play a little trick on her and had reversed her mirror, so that on this particular morning Enyadatta saw no reflection of her face. This threw her into a state of panic: she could not find her head!

Enyadatta began shouting, "Where is my head? Where is my head?" She searched under the bed, beneath the bedclothes, in the closet, behind the bureau, and all over the house with no success. Then she ran out of her house in a frenzy, trying to retrace her steps of the previous night (when she had had a bit too much to drink) while continuing to scream, "Where is my head?"

Finally a friend saw Enyadatta dashing around half-crazed and managed to catch hold of her. He tried to reason with her, telling her over and over again that she had not lost her head, that it was still on her shoulders. But in her confused state, she could not believe or even really hear what he was saying. Her friend had to tie her down to a chair so that she could not run around and hurt herself or anybody else. She continued to shriek and cry, fighting to free herself from the confinement of the ropes, desperately trying to continue the search for her head. Finally she slumped over, limp and exhausted.

Only now, as she began to relax out of sheer fatigue, was Enyadatta able to hear what her friend was saying, but she still could not accept it. She began to ask herself, "Am I really missing my head or have I been deceiving myself?" At just the right moment her friend slapped her across the face. Grabbing her head, she screamed out in pain, "Ouch! My head, my head, you hurt my head!" Then she exclaimed, "My head? . . . My head! I have my head!" She realized in that instant without any doubt that she indeed had her head.

Enyadatta was overjoyed. She started shouting, "Look everyone, I have found my head! What a marvelous thing!" Seeing her in this overexcited state of joyful relief, her friend decided to leave her tied up until she came to her senses.

Enyadatta eventually saw the absurdity of the whole situation, that she had never really lost her head. She returned home, took care of her family, and went about her work, but now she was not as self-involved as before. Because of this experience, she was no longer so vain or self-centered.

The original version of this tale as told by Shakyamuni Buddha is recorded in the *Lotus Sutra* and presents one of the best analogies to our life. The stage before Enyadatta looked into the mirror is the point where all of us start before we begin to question what is lacking. We are all very busy trying to find security and happiness, to gain position, name, reputation, and wealth. We are completely self-involved and busy with the superficial appearances of things, how others see us and what they think of us. Then at some point we begin to think that something is lacking; our life feels empty and we start searching for some truth or meaning to it.

We begin looking for the truth, running here and there, trying to improve our lives through various ways to find the answer. Hopefully, on our own or with the help of a spiritual friend, we begin a sitting practice. At first we may find it difficult to be immobile and to quiet the mind. We find lots of resistance and discomfort, but if we are truly determined to find our head, our true nature, we continue the practice of sitting. Even though we may hear or read that we are not lacking anything, that we all have Buddha-nature, we simply cannot accept this until we have exhausted our searching through practice. Only then can we begin to hear the teaching.

At this point we trust that we have the potential to awaken to our true nature. The actual awakening can come at any moment by a slap in the face, the cawing of a bird, or the sound of a thunderclap. In that moment, forgetting ourself, our true nature is revealed. Now, experiencing the great joy and excitement of having awakened to our Buddha-nature, we fall into the "stink of Zen." We want to share this experience with everybody. This phase can continue for many years until we are able to drop our notion of specialness. For, just like Enyadatta, we have never been without our Buddha-nature, so what is so special about finding it? We must finally come to recognize that all has been a self-deception, thinking that we were missing it and then thinking that we have found it.

Only at this point of having dropped the attachment to our awakening are we able to return to ordinary mind, no longer searching for anything to make us better or more whole, just being ourselves, doing whatever it is we need to do, taking care of whatever situation arises. We are now less self-involved and more aware of everything in the environment. We see things as they really are and function freely out of true compassion and wisdom.

As in the parable of Enyadatta, we must search for our heads in order to realize we have never lost them. If you have really lost your head, how do you search for it? With complete resolve, in a state of utter panic and desperation, as if your head were on fire! With that kind of determination you are sure to realize your true nature. Hold back to protect yourself just a little, even a hair's breadth, and you cannot do it.

Why do you think that so few people have attained enlightenment throughout the ages? Because the first thing we have to do, the very first thing, not the last step, is to cast off attachment to the body and mind. All the great masters who sought the Way with *bodhi*-mind paid no heed to themselves and let body and mind drop. This is the first thing we must do also: drop body and mind. When? We say, "Let us do it in a couple of years; why do it now? There are so many things we can do now that are more important." What do we lose when we drop body and mind? Absolutely nothing, except a lot of ideas and concepts, likes and dislikes, hate and anger, jealously and envy and greed. And what replaces all that? Compassion, unconditional love, Truth!

> *Just let things be in their own way*
> *and there will be neither coming nor going.*

When we sit in zazen, is this not what we are doing, just letting everything be in its own way? That is what is so beautiful about it. When we go to sleep, in a sense we are doing this also, but we are not aware. Sitting is the only time we let things just be with full awareness. And I do not mean sitting limited to the cushion, but any time you are attentive and open, even in movement. Allowing everything to be as it is, that is true sitting: allowing whatever wants to come up simply to come up and pass away—birds chirping, sun rising, moon setting, clouds drifting, dogs barking, cats yowling. Do not create any barrier or set yourself apart. When you are sitting: woof, woof! There is no distinction between you and the dog: just woof, woof! No outside or inside; no stopping or starting; no coming or going; no distance, no separation. But what do we do? Right away we place it "out there" and name it "barking dog."

The fact that you can distinguish between a cat yowling and a dog barking means you have *prajna,* discriminating wisdom. Before we learn how to think in a nondual way, our distinctions are called discriminating delusion, discriminating mind. We hear "dog" or "cat" and right away our preferences come up: "I love dogs, I hate cats," or vice versa; or "I love dogs in the right place, but not outside the window barking."

When you simply distinguish a cat from a dog, that is *prajna.* As soon as you start holding preferences, that is discriminating delusion. Just let everything be. Allow the cats to yowl, the dogs to bark, the cars to drive by. We are always trying to control our environment, but in sitting we do not; we cannot do anything about it. With our spouses, our children, our parents, that is what we try to do all the time: control and dominate. Be with others as you are when you sit: let people be in their own way.

7 Obey Your Own Nature

Obey the nature of things
and you will walk freely and undisturbed.
When thought is in bondage the truth is hidden,
for everything is murky and unclear.
The burdensome practice of judging
brings annoyance and weariness.
What benefit can be derived
from distinctions and separations?

Obey the nature of things
and you will walk freely and undisturbed.

How can we obey what we do not even know, what we do not even realize, what we are not intimate with? The answer is simple: we cannot. That is precisely the cause of our suffering, the cause of our problems and our feelings of alienation.

Enlightenment is to see into the nature of all things and into the nature of the self. What is that nature? What is your nature, my nature, our nature? That is called emptiness, suchness, *mu*, Buddha-nature, true nature. And what is this Buddha-nature or true nature? No-nature! That is our true nature. Isn't that interesting? Our nature is no-nature. Our true self is no-self. Our true mind is no-mind. Our true essence of mind is no-essence, no-thingness.

What is it that we are always attempting to do? To define ourselves in relationship to everything and everyone. I am a mother or father in relation to children; a child, a son, a daughter in relation to parents; husband in relation to wife; lover in relation to beloved; criminal in relation to society. Liar, thief, bad person, good person: it all involves relationship. And what do we do with these definitions? We bind ourselves. How? The very act of definition itself creates a boundary.

To begin with, it is just One Mind, all One; then we generate all the boundaries and definitions. As soon as we define ourselves in relation to another we feel more comfortable, because now we know how to be and to act. To go into a situation completely ignorant of our role is very scary. We really have to trust ourselves then. But how can we trust if we do not know who we are? So we fall back on some definition of ourselves and put our trust in that.

This seems pretty flimsy, doesn't it, to put my trust in a definition? Look what happens if I define myself as a son, if that is how I create my psychological security: eventually mother and father die. Now who am I? If I create my identity as a wife and lose my husband, then who am I? If I am a parent and I lose my child, who am I then? If I define myself as a child, then I turn nineteen or twenty and leave home, who am I?

We lose our identity when we lose our definition. We do not realize it, but that is a wonderful, extraordinary happening, because for a time we are free of our boundaries. For a moment we are *nobody*, but that is just too frightening. So in order to grab on to some definition, a false sense of security and comfort, what do we do right away? We get into another relationship. At least in a relationship, even if it is not working for us, we know who we are.

Then we sit down on the cushion. What happens right away? We start losing these boundaries, these notions of who we are. We start losing our identity. The same thing happens in a relationship with someone who does not clearly define us, one who just accepts us without judgment. Then who are we? Instead of staying open and living without boundary, we close down in fear of the unknown, restricting and confining ourselves within a familiar self-definition.

We do not like to live in fear, in fact we hate it, but that is precisely what we do. I do not want to say to myself, "I am afraid," so instead I turn it outward: "I hate you." But we do not like saying that because in this society it is not OK to hate, is it? It may be OK to get angry, but not to hate. So we either walk around getting angry all the time or we suppress that anger and then we are frustrated and upset. What is under the anger? Hatred. And what is under the hatred? Fear. And what is under that fear? No definition: no-self. What is the cause of the problem? Lack of faith in no-self or no fixed self: the self without a firm definition.

You see this while working on such koans as *mu* or "Who is the master?" or "Who hears the sound?" It is obvious: I hear the sound. Who else hears it? If you say you hear, still I am hearing. Three million people say they hear it, still just one I is hearing. That is what is called universal "I," limitless Mind. If a dog barks, every one of us hears it. If we ask, "Who hears it?", I hear it. Within that big I we create little circles, little I's. It is as if these little circles were rubbing against each other like stones in a river: "Close the door!" "No! I want the door open." "Well, I want it closed." "Too bad, I want it open!" "Leave it closed!" "No, open!" We forget that the real problem is not whether the door is open or closed, whether the children eat this or eat that. The real problem is our separation from one another, the defining of separate selves to give us a false sense of security, a false identity.

This practice is all about losing that false identity. Many of us have spent years in therapy to gain a solid sense of self. How can we live with no identity? Freely! Undisturbed, like water. Water has three states. If we heat water, it turns into a gas. That is like our true nature. In its very essence, it is like a gas, or clear space: no fixed boundaries, free. Then it cools and condenses, becoming liquid. Now we can see it and touch it, but still it can flow in all directions. When we freeze it, the flow stops, it becomes a chunk of ice.

Guess which state we like to abide in? A solid identity, edges defined, like ice. We know where we end, we know where we begin. We are a clear-cut object. But as water or as gas we have no clear definition. Our biggest fear as a chunk of ice is losing our identity. And yet we are constantly getting chipped and hurt and broken. I have heard an expression, "We made love like two ice cubes," that fits perfectly. Here we are, trying to have a relationship like two chunks of ice and all we can do is bump into each other, all because we are so afraid of melting, losing our false identities.

What is a relationship? Becoming one, melting back into our true nature. Yet losing our identity and merging into another is the very thing we resist most strongly. We spend all our time guarding that identity, protecting it. What are we afraid of? That somebody is going to abuse us, misuse or take advantage of us? God forbid that we be taken advantage of!

Again, what is our practice all about? To offer this life up. To whom? To the whole, to the Dharma. Give up your life! That is a true offering. We offer incense; what is that incense? It represents our life. We offer bows; we are offering up our very life. What is the Buddhadharma, the whole? Everyone. Everything. So offer your life to everyone, to everything. "But," we say, "they might take advantage of me." When you offer your life, you must offer it freely, no strings attached. It is not really an offering if you are holding back, saying, "I will only offer if you don't take advantage of me." Just give it!

What is true giving, *dana paramita*? Giving ourselves up completely, giving ourselves away totally; that is the most difficult thing to do. It is easy to give money, easiest thing in the world; it really costs you nothing. But giving your life away, giving up your life, that is true giving! *Dana paramita* means to offer your life, to relinquish this body and mind. To whom? To anyone who wants to use it. Then body and mind no longer belong to you anymore. You lose your identity. You literally don't know who you are. You still have a name, but it is not even *your* name anymore.

Now your life is the life of the Buddhadharma; your body is the Buddha body. Then your life becomes a reality, but it is not yours anymore! You cannot own or possess it; every time you try, you feel terrible because you are stopping the natural order, which is to flow. You are going against that basic law, "Obey the nature of things and you will walk freely and undisturbed." So obey your true nature, which is no-nature, no fixed self.

We are afraid to lose our own individual identity, but the more we resist losing it the more we suffer. It is a very simple equation: resistance breeds persistence. The more we resist, the more we persist. So let it go! Don't be like a monkey. Have you heard how they capture monkeys in India? First they take a coconut and hollow it out. Then they anchor down the bottom, cut a small opening in the top, and put something sweet inside. The monkey comes along, reaches in and grabs the sweet. Then the monkey tries to yank its hand out, but can't without letting go of the sweet. Its hand is stuck and that monkey would rather lose its life than let go. Of course, the monkey doesn't know it is losing its life. Like us, it is just hanging on to what it desires. It will become somebody's monkey-brain soup only because it is unwilling to stop clinging. We hold on just as tightly to our identity, creating all kinds of suffering and conflict. Let it go! Just open your hand and you will be filled with the Dharma.

> *When thought is in bondage the truth is hidden,*
> *for everything is murky and unclear.*

Our mind is not free when we cling to thoughts and feelings instead of allowing them to come and go by themselves. Don't chase after them! You can just observe them. Let them come and go. As long as you don't cling to them, it is fine to have plenty of thoughts and ideas. There is nothing wrong with that; maybe the more the better. But don't get stuck in a one-sided perspective, such as: my ideas are right, his ideas are wrong; my ideas are good, his ideas are bad.

One aspect of koan study is to be able to step out of your own shoes and get a different perspective, to turn around, step into the other's shoes, and take a fresh look. Forget yourself. Become the shitting cow or the oak tree or the blade of grass. But you can't do this as long as you cling to your own self-concept, physical shape, and boundaries. So drop your identity, your self-consciousness. Then, undisturbed and unhindered, you can be anything.

Everything is murky and unclear when the Truth is hidden. What is this Truth? There is only one Truth. Call it God, if you will, but what is God? As John Lennon said, it is just a concept. Anything we define as *it* is not it. So let go of all concepts and all definitions. There is only the One, what we call Truth, reality, God, Buddha, Buddha-nature, true self, *mu*.

And what is this One? It is your life: just One Mind. And what is this One Mind? *This!* This very self. But what is this self that is "I?" Undefinable, unrealizable, unattainable: vast emptiness, limitless space. That is your life, with no beginning, no birth; therefore with no end, no death. This unborn nature is coming into being every instant, more than sixty-four thousand times a second. In order for it to be born every moment, it must also die every moment. That is what this life really is, being born and dying every moment, faster than we can see. When you are really mindful, life is like a moving picture in slow motion, each frame a separate and complete moment. At normal speed the film gives the illusion of movement, making us believe that things are really happening in our lives.

Our minds can never grasp this: on the one hand life is unborn and undying and on the other it is being born and dying every moment. It is a paradox, like light being both wave and particle at the same time or like my theory that the universe is expanding and contracting simultaneously. Scientists have been debating whether the universe is expanding or contracting. Suppose it is both expanding and contracting, like going into a black hole. When you get sucked into a black hole, do you contract or expand? Or are you blown in and out simultaneously? Our true nature is like a black hole. If we really empty ourselves, anyone who comes close gets sucked into our open space. Become like a big suction, a great vacuum.

> *The burdensome practice of judging*
> *brings annoyance and weariness.*

Isn't it true? Isn't sitting there all the time judging yourself and others tiring, exhausting? "I'm no good, I'm always messing up. My sitting is no good; I fall asleep. I have too many thoughts,

I'm not doing well enough, I'm not trying hard enough." The only thing that separates us from Buddha is that the Buddha doesn't find fault. When there are thoughts, there are thoughts. When there are no thoughts, there are no thoughts. When there is judgment, there is judgment. When there is no judgment, no judgment. Why judge the judger? Why condemn yourself all the time? Let yourself be! Let the true nature of things just be, then everything passes away naturally.

So when you sit, what is there to do? Only just sit. Stop trying to change it, correct it, improve it. Sometimes it is great, sometimes not. Great sitting is great sitting and bad sitting is also great sitting. Just sit. It is so wearisome to keep judging. And what about judging others? No one is going to live up to our standards and it doesn't matter anyway, because everyone is OK, just perfect the way they are.

We feel free to say, "Oh, you need psychological help! Better go see a shrink." Yet if someone says that to us, our reaction is, "Oh! What are you talking about?" The Native Americans had a positive attitude toward crazy people. When people acted insane, the Native Americans thought they were possessed by spirits acting through them. Children and psychotics, enlightened people and drunkards, all are unpredictable. That is their wisdom. And whom don't we like? Who scares us? Drunkards, enlightened people, psychotics, and young kids! Of course, you are thinking, "We can't *really* be afraid of young kids"—but what do we do with them? We lock them up. If they act wild, what do we say? "Go to your room! Close the door! Go to school! I can't take you anymore. At least for three hours I get a rest."

It is hard being around someone unpredictable, someone really free, like Maezumi Roshi. You never know what he is going to do next. One minute he is kind and compassionate and the next moment he is ready to chew your head off! When we were visiting Trungpa Rinpoche's Dharma center in London just after Trungpa's death, Roshi was asked to give a talk. During his life, Trungpa used to emphasize strongly that Buddhism is a nontheistic religion. Addressing Trungpa Rinpoche's students on his forty-ninth memorial day, Roshi gave a superb talk about Nietzsche, declaring that definitely there is a God; that he, Roshi, believes in God; that Nietzsche was nuts to claim "God is dead"; and that God was doing fine, but something had died in Nietzsche.

Then Roshi went to give a talk in France and a very devout Catholic asked him about God. Roshi said, "No God! I don't believe in God!" Two students who were with me at both talks were shocked. One of them said, "What do you mean, 'No God'? Just a few days ago you declared your belief in God!" Roshi just laughed. He is utterly free, unpredictable, not sticking anywhere, not attaching to anything. God, no God: just concepts.

Go far beyond such dualistic discrimination as enlightened or deluded, good or bad. One day someone says, "Oh, you are so good, so wonderful!" and you puff yourself up; then the next day, "Oh, you are a terrible person!" and you feel miserable. What difference does it make? Just labels! You are what you are. The tree doesn't care what you call it, an enlightened or a deluded tree. A tree is a tree. Why can't we be like that? Just as we are, undefinable and without the label of good or bad, enlightened or not, Buddha or sentient being. All hogwash. Be free!

What benefit can be derived from distinctions and separations?

Such distinctions as me and you, good and bad, right and wrong, life and death. Why worry about death or life? When we are alive, we are alive. When we are dead, we are dead. Why not just take care of this moment? There is no tomorrow. There is no yesterday. There is not even today, just this very moment.

You are nothing, and if you really put your faith in this nothing you cannot be disappointed. If you put your faith in something, then you become dependent on it and when you lose it you fall flat on your face. So please, have deep faith in your true nature, your indefinable no-self, and be truly free.

8 Strive to No Goals

> If you wish to move in the One Way
> do not dislike even the world of senses and ideas.
> Indeed, to accept them fully
> is identical with true Enlightenment.
> The wise man strives to no goals
> but the foolish man fetters himself.
> There is one Dharma, not many;
> distinctions arise from the clinging needs of the
>   ignorant.
> To seek Mind with discriminating mind
> is the greatest of all mistakes.

If you wish to move in the One Way
do not dislike even the world of senses and ideas.

Anything we dislike, anything we try to suppress will become a hindrance in our practice. We have ideas that certain things are good and others evil; for instance, studying Buddhism we may get the idea that being attached to the senses is bad and being unattached is good. Then when certain feelings, thoughts, attractive visual images arise, we accuse ourselves of attachment and call ourselves bad. If we cannot be affected in any way by these sense objects, then we call that good and positive. Now we think we can live a pure, undefiled life.

But that is already erroneous thinking arising from our dualistic, discriminating consciousness. This is bad, that is good; this is wrong, that is right. How can we live in the world of the senses without making such distinctions and still be one with the Way?

The answer is simple, of course, but that does not mean it is easy to do: cut off the entire discriminating mind. When you cut off this dualistic mind, all your aversions and preferences, then you become one with your life, one with the Way.

Therefore, as attachments arise, don't take a position for or against them. Just notice them. Just be aware. That is the key word: aware. We call it *anuttara samyak sambodhi*: supreme, unsurpassable awareness. Whatever we have to do, just do it. Whatever is appropriate at the moment, just be one with it. When we are simply aware, we have that option. When we are not aware, then we are dragged around by all our desires, our clinging. We are not even conscious of what is happening.

How do we become aware? Zazen. When we sit and simply accept whatever is arising, then that is *anuttara samyak sambodhi*. Just allow whatever arises to come up and let it pass by without clinging to it. Be like the vast, empty sky. Or, as Yasutani Roshi used to say, be like a clean white sheet of paper. Whatever is written on that sheet of paper is neither good nor bad, but our normal way is to evaluate it. Whatever comes up, we are always judging: "These are bad, evil thoughts; I should have only positive thoughts."

As soon as we think like that, of course, we fall into discriminating mind and then we get into trouble. We start suppressing and repressing things. We start searching for certain kinds of thoughts, seeking only good thoughts. Then we become our own worst enemy. Whatever thoughts come up, accept them fully, even thoughts of sensual desire. If you see a beautiful woman or a handsome man and you feel sexually attracted, just accept it, don't suppress it. Through your total acceptance, you avoid being victimized. You are the boss, you are the master. But as soon as you try to suppress it because you don't like what is coming up, you become the victim of your disowned desire. Then you feel like you are being dragged around by your senses and attachments and are no longer in control.

When we feel we have lost control, we try to regain it. But that doesn't work, so what do we do next? We try to control others. If we are in a position of power anyway, then we just control everybody and they accept it because we are supposed to be in charge. But when we don't have political power, we may start controlling our children, our wife, our dog, our friends, anyone we see as weaker than us. At this point control can be a real problem; we become little dictators.

It all stems from not liking what arises—being attached to certain ideas of what is a good thing, clinging to our own views, our own opinions. We don't realize that they are just our own ideas; we take them for granted. We always think that our beliefs and ideas are right and everybody else's are wrong. If they share our views, then of course we say that they are smart, they understand.

For example, if we think nuclear bombs and nuclear power are bad, then those who share that view must have wisdom and those who do not are stupid. In Maine we had a vote on whether or not to eliminate the nuclear power plant. About sixty percent of the people voted to keep the plant, so do we say these people are stupid and the other forty percent are wise? That is how we think, while those who are for nuclear power feel we are against them: "They don't understand our plight. They don't see how that will put us out of business. We need low-cost power for our livelihood."

In our practice we have to learn not to be stuck in any position. As soon as we get stuck, we lose our objectivity and effectiveness. We become helpless, useless. Look at the mess the world is in and it all stems from this: being stuck. If everybody on this planet could see objectively from all perspectives, there would be no reason for wars. There would be no reason to be for or against any group. We could live in harmony and peace.

Things may sometimes appear to change outwardly, but we are still not at peace inwardly, not in harmony; we still have wars within ourselves. For example, we want to eat a lot of food and really fill ourselves up, then we oppose ourselves: "Oh, I shouldn't do that," and the conflict starts. Or we want to possess something or somebody, then right away we say to ourselves, "I shouldn't feel like that," and the war is on. With battles going on constantly in our minds, how can we bring any kind of peace into the world?

Our practice is how to go beyond pros and cons, how to go beyond likes and dislikes. But how do we really transcend the dichotomies our minds are always creating? The answer, of course, is to sit zazen. What is true zazen? Letting go of the attachment to body and mind. Which mind? Discriminating mind, dualistic mind: let it go! Why do we cling to it so much? Because it gives us a sense of identity. "I like this and I hate that" and "I am for this and I am against that": this is how I know who I am.

"I am a Democrat." "I am a socialist." "I am a Republican." "I am an artist." "I am a thinker." "I am a jock." "I am sensitive and tough, macho but vulnerable—good, clean, pure." Who are we without these labels? When you really let go of all the pros and cons, who are you then? Drop all your likes and dislikes, notions of career and position; then who is left? "God, I don't know . . . I am nobody, I am nothing."

That is how we feel, but it isn't true. When we really let go, we become everything. At that point we are identified with all things: the flower, the oak tree, the morning star.

Indeed, to accept them fully
is identical with true Enlightenment.

Being attached to sensations is samsara, the wheel of suffering. Now here he says that samsara is identical with enlightenment. What nonsense! How can the samsaric world, this suffering world, be identical with true enlightenment?

I sit long hours on my cushion seeking to be enlightened, to free myself from suffering. Buddha said life is suffering, the cause of that suffering is desire and attachment, and the way out of that suffering is to follow the Eightfold Path. The first step on the path is right understanding, to realize that our upside-down, perverted view of reality—separating ourselves from the rest of the world—is the cause of our attachments. And what is this Way that is beyond suffering? Our dualistic mind thinks that to be free from suffering means to get rid of suffering. No. We can never get rid of anything. As soon as we think we have gotten rid of something, it pops up again and we find out it is still there.

When I first began practicing at the Zen Center of Los Angeles in 1972, I thought sexual desire would never control me again. As soon as I decided that, guess what happened? One weekend I found myself so completely controlled by my desire that I drove a hundred miles north from Los Angeles to Santa Barbara just to seek out an old girlfriend. When I discovered she was now happily married, I turned around and drove a hundred fifty miles south to Orange County to find another old girlfriend!

As soon as we think that we are rid of something, then that is the very dragon which pokes its head up, breathing fire. We can't get rid of anything; all we can do is include it, accept it, make friends with it. Accept and include even your suffering. When you are sitting and you have pain in your legs, in your back, in your head, accept it—maybe even enjoy it. How can we enjoy pain? We must be masochists! Yet we may discover that pain can be our most intimate friend.

Remember Buddha's first teaching: life is suffering. Life is identical to suffering and suffering is identical to life. If you had no suffering you wouldn't have life. When there is no suffering, you are dead. Just think about it: the closer you are to not having any suffering, the more numb you are. When you are ultimately numb, you are dead. You can't feel anything, not even joy. Be thankful you can feel. Of course, some of those feelings are unpleasant. What we do is attach to the pleasant ones; we seek after the pleasant ones and try to avoid the unpleasant ones, and that becomes our basic problem.

One time I was wondering why I do the things I do. When I am sitting there by myself, why do I get up? If I am standing still, why do I move? So I decided to do an experiment: to stand still until I knew why I moved. Forty minutes later I found out: it was very uncomfortable. Try it. Sit there two or three hours and see why you finally move.

Then I realized that this is the way my whole life goes. Only the process is usually more subtle and sometimes I am not aware of it. Then I was keenly aware; I was watching every moment:

"OK, what's going to make me move now?" I realized how I was seeking after comfort, trying to avoid pain. That is what we are doing all the time. We are sitting there, constantly adjusting our posture, trying to be a little more comfortable. Some of us are more subtle: not merely adjusting our posture, we are adjusting our heads, too: "If I can just attune my mind a little better, everything will be pleasant."

But what happens when we truly just accept it all, just let everything be? Then there is chaos. Great! I love chaos. Confusion? I love confusion. Ever since I realized how much I love chaos and confusion, I haven't been able to be confused. I keep seeking it, keep asking for it: "God, give me some chaos!" Now, even when I want to be an agent of chaos and confusion, I can't be.

Try the same thing with being burdened. If you are overburdened or exploited, invite the burden and the exploitation. Invite everybody to exploit you. That is what a Bodhisattva is. The Bodhisattva invites everybody, "Exploit me! Use me as the welcome mat to the front door. Wipe your feet on me." Isn't that an unpleasant thought, to be like a welcome mat, and everybody that walks through that door is going to step on you, wipe their feet on you, clean themselves off on you?

One master when asked, "What is Buddha?" said, "A shit stick," another form of welcome mat. In the old days people used a stick instead of toilet paper, so he is saying that Buddha is something to wipe yourself with. Become that and you are Buddha. That is what you are really seeking, not some guy sitting there like a pure lotus flower with a halo. Since the shit stick is the real Buddha, if you want to aspire to something, aspire to be a shit stick, a doormat. What kind of idiot does that? A Bodhisattva. The Bodhisattva says, "I am here, use me, even if it is to wipe your ass!"

We aspire to get out of our pain and suffering, to be enlightened, to be clear, to be a Buddha. A Bodhisattva is one who has already realized he is Buddha and, becoming a Buddha, he also recognizes that everybody is Buddha, everything is Buddha. Then he naturally feels concern for all the numberless beings who are

Buddhas but don't realize it yet. What good is Buddhahood to them if they don't recognize it? In his compassion, the Bodhisattva declares, "Rather than dwell in joy, in serenity, in utter freedom, I give it all up to become a shit stick, a doormat, a servant of others. I will remain deluded in order to save all sentient beings."

Can you make that kind of vow? Can you vow to be deluded, to save all sentient beings before you attain ultimate, complete liberation? Well, what is so hard about it? You already are deluded. Why not just accept it, be it? It is so much easier, because then you don't have to seek anything. You don't have to try to become anything that you are not. You can just be one with your true self. What is your true self? Mine is deluded, full of attachments and desires. What about yours?

But wait a minute, that is called our ego self. The true self is supposed to be free of all that. Is there a true self and a false self? Must be. Isn't that what we are aspiring toward, to realize our true self and get rid of our false self? But isn't that discriminating mind? To seek enlightenment, to seek Mind with the discriminating mind? Isn't that what we are trying to do to become enlightened? And he is saying it is all foolishness! Doesn't that mean that we are utterly stupid? That is what we are, so we might as well be completely stupid! But then what? What do I do then? Why am I here? What else is there to do but just sit? But without a goal?

> *The wise man strives to no goals*
> *but the foolish man fetters himself.*

Fetters himself with what? With the goal of becoming enlightened, free from suffering. The wise man has no goal, aspires to no-goal, has the goal of no-goal. What is that called? *Shikantaza*. Just to sit, without looking for anything, with no goal or purpose. Then we are just sitting in the midst of delusion, utterly and completely one with our delusion. That is how we go beyond enlightenment and delusion.

From the very beginning I have never been fettered, never been bound by anything, I have always been as free as the clouds in the sky, I just didn't realize it. I thought I had to get someplace to be free, attain something to be free, realize something to be free; or at least get rid of something to be free, such as my delusions, my preferences, my attachments. Then I would be enlightened. No, then I would just be stupid, caught up in dualistic thinking.

> *There is one Dharma, not many;*
> *distinctions arise from the clinging needs of the ignorant.*

There is only one Dharma, one Truth, one reality. What is that one reality? We can say it in many ways: *This*, just *this*, your life, your self, things as they are. And what do we do with things as they are? We try to change them, make them different, make them better. We have likes and dislikes, aversions and attachments, but there is only one Truth, one Dharma. Many different truths cannot be the absolute Truth. Those are only truths in a relative sense.

The one Dharma is not dual, not two. When you live at one with yourself, one with the environment, one with the Way, one with the Dharma, you are living that Truth, being that Truth. This means not excluding anything, not avoiding anything. Whatever comes up, that is your karma, so face it, be it, be one with it. If you are depressed, be depressed. Happy, be happy. Stuck, be stuck. Be completely stuck! Deluded, be deluded. Wise? Be wise.

None of it lasts. It is changing all the time, isn't it? One moment we are wise, the next moment stupid: that is the way of the enlightened person. That is what our ultimate aim is in Zen practice: to be the great fool, the joker. The joker is wild. And what power the joker has: to be anything, a king, a deuce, a queen, a jack; to have complete flexibility, fluidity, oneness with the situation; to be really free, so free that one is able to be detached, free even to be deluded, to be unwise.

Can you imagine how painful and tough it would be, trying to be wise all the time? Thank God none of us try. Or trying to be good and pure all the time: Sir Lancelot or Mother Teresa? What a burden! I am sure Mother Teresa doesn't try to be good. She just does what she has to do. That is the secret of great people, they just do what they have to do.

We all have a function: the heart has a function, the liver has a function, the gall bladder has a function, you have a function. The heart can't be the gall bladder, the gall bladder can't be the heart. When the gall bladder tries to be the heart, the body has a problem. If Genpo tries to be somebody else, if somebody else tries to be Genpo, then we both have a problem.

> *To seek Mind with discriminating mind*
> *is the greatest of all mistakes.*

Discriminating mind is the one that hates this and loves that, wants this and doesn't want that, seeks this and runs away from that. How can the discriminating mind, which arises from the very stupidity of clinging, ever free itself from suffering, from delusion, from attachments, no matter how hard it struggles? The whole problem is that this stupid, ignorant mind doesn't realize it is already free. To seek enlightenment while clinging to discriminating mind is utterly ridiculous!

9 *All Dualities Are Like Dreams*

Rest and unrest derive from illusion;
with enlightenment there is no liking and disliking.
All dualities come from ignorant inference.
They are like dreams of flowers in air:
foolish to try to grasp them.
Gain and loss, right and wrong:
such thoughts must finally be abolished at once.

Rest and unrest derive from illusion;
with enlightenment there is no liking and disliking.

There are five major attachments: the first one is to rest; the second is to food and drink; the third one is to sex; the fourth is to fame and position; and the fifth one is to gain or wealth. When we are awakened to *prajna*, then our attachment to the desires drops off.

It goes something like this: when you practice strongly, as in a long retreat, you do not get much sleep or very much to eat and not much is going on to entertain you. By just following the schedule, you learn that you can get along fine without much rest, food, or amusement. When you live like this, in time the other attachments drop away also. But you have to do it totally; for instance, if there is only a certain amount of tiredness and a certain amount of concentration power built up, then as soon as you stop and get enough rest, right away desire comes back.

As long as you are practicing intensely, even though the

attachment to wealth or money may be very strong, it will drop away. You won't care anything about money; you are thinking, "Just give me some good food and some sleep, and maybe a little sex!" Then as you are practicing longer and getting more tired and more hungry, even attachment to fame or name or position drops. But for a while it is still there in the form of desire for or aversion to assigned positions within the retreat, as for instance, wanting to be the teacher's personal attendant rather than the cook.

As we keep going in the practice, that attachment also drops off, yet still there is desire for sex: all kinds of sexual fantasies, energies, and urges come up. But if you are really exhausted, even that falls away. You are too tired and too hungry even to think about sex.

As you continue to practice strongly, next comes food, a big issue in the monastery, as it is everywhere else. Even when the food is bad (in some monasteries it is awful), there is still the issue of quantity. The worse the food is, the more we want, because it is not really satisfying. In a Japanese monastery you may get just some white rice and a few pickles. Some monks take three or four bowls of white rice, like hungry ghosts trying desperately to stop their craving with food that cannot satisfy.

Finally, even desire for food drops and all we want is rest: "Just give me a bed to lie down in!" That is why in some traditions, in order to cut the attachment to all desires, people never lie down. In some places they sit all night with a chin rest that is supported on their hands, while robe straps tie up their legs in a cross-legged position. Of course they may doze, but they can't fall over and lose their posture. At a Chinese temple in California, there are people who sleep in a box. The box is about as wide as a meditation mat but too short to lie down in. They sit all night and anyone who falls over just hits against the box, since there is no way to lie down without curling up completely. I imagine it is very uncomfortable, but I have seen it done.

As long as we get enough rest, then the other desires come up. That is one reason that in very intensive retreats only three to four hours of sleep are permitted at night. But in this verse the

Third Patriarch is saying that both rest and unrest are basically illusory and in enlightenment no liking or disliking need arise toward either one; so we must look at the other side, too: why should we dislike rest? What is wrong with rest? Nothing is wrong with it: when you are tired, rest. From our point of view, the tradition at the Chinese temple not to lie down is too extreme, too ascetic. It is not well balanced. When asked, "What is Zen?" many of the masters would say, "When I am tired, I rest; when I am hungry, I eat." We need not go too far; we should neither avoid lack of rest nor be stuck on getting no rest.

> *All dualities come from ignorant inference.*
> *They are like dreams of flowers in air:*
> *foolish to try to grasp them.*

Ignorant inference is common with all of us: we understand something and then we begin to jump to conclusions. We start adding to what we know, inferring all kinds of things from it, and soon we have constructed a whole scenario that has nothing to do with reality. We have created it all in our heads. Through our dualistic minds we infer things about ourselves, too, and about our lives. It is so difficult somehow for us just to take things as they are without adding something extra; so hard to see ourselves clearly, to see someone else clearly, to see any situation clearly. Always we want to add something or take something away.

> *Gain and loss, right and wrong:*
> *such thoughts must finally be abolished at once.*

We are always doing something with a selfish motive. The key is how to practice with no thought of gaining, not seeking or wanting something either from our practice or from what we do or give. So often when we give, it is not real giving. We give something to someone and right away we want something back in return.

This self-centered expectation is deeply rooted in our consciousness, especially because we go through a standard system of education that strongly engenders that attitude. You run across that way of thinking much less with simple folk; but with the most highly educated, it is the worst. If I go to college for four years or to university for eight years to get a Ph.D. or M.D. or law degree, and I do it because I want status and money, then the attitude naturally arises that I deserve something for my effort. Because of all my hard work, I deserve to earn a high salary at the very least—I am entitled to it!

That is the attitude of the acquisitive mind and it affects everything we do: "If I give something, I deserve something back," and "If I give you something, I want to own you, possess you." We have a wonderful home, but it is not enough, so we need a wonderful car. An ordinary car isn't enough, though—it has to be a Mercedes.

This kind of acquisitive mind is what we develop in our educational system. We always do everything for a reason. Can you imagine: every time you shit, it has to be for a reason? As Kodo Sawaki Roshi said, "You don't eat in order to shit. You don't shit in order to make manure. But nowadays people go to high school in order to get to college and go to college in order to get a good job." Then we can make more money, so we can have a better position and higher status in the community. Buy more! Own more! It is so American. And this can be our attitude even about Zen.

Dana, true giving, means to give without expecting anything in return. Not seeking anything, not looking for anything, we just give. If we give to benefit ourselves, that is not giving, that is buying or bartering. We must give with no strings attached. The idea that we must get something back for whatever we give is so strong that in the East the concept developed of gaining merit through *dana*, that from selfless giving we can at the very least expect to get some delayed merit. We may not get something material in this lifetime, but perhaps in the next lifetime we will be rewarded—basically the same attitude of gaining something through our so-called giving, just a bit more subtle.

When it comes to the Buddhadharma, there really is nothing to seek. Our zazen itself *is* the Buddhadharma. Thus we need not practice with a seeking attitude, with the idea of gaining something. We should not despise the boredom that arises in zazen nor try to avoid it, but just practice with our whole heart, without looking for some kind of completion or attainment. This is the right attitude that is in accord with the principle of nonseeking.

Sitting itself is nondualistic; in zazen there is no barrier between the self and all phenomena. Zazen is the true form of the self. But if you are sitting expecting results, it is not true zazen. We can say true sitting is to realize the Way, but actually true zazen *is* the realization itself. And what is this realization of the Way? That when you sit, the koan of true self, Buddha-nature, Buddhadharma, the Buddha Way is in realization.

Once we realize the Way, it is not limited to sitting; everything we do from morning to night is nothing but the Way. But until we realize this Way, nothing we do is really the Way. And if we imagine that we have attained the Way, we can get stuck there. This then becomes another form of delusion.

If we are looking only from the absolute side, there is just the absolute. Then everything is nothing and there is no way to be ignorant, deluded. Even being deluded and not realizing the Way is enlightenment: nothing to do, nothing to seek for. But if we are stuck on the relative side, as soon as I say "nothing to do," then what comes up? "So why do it? Why practice? Why sit, why get so tired and have sore legs, sore knees? What am I doing this for?" The acquisitive mind leads us astray, to do everything for the sake of gaining something. Why is it so difficult to drop the acquisitive mind? Why is it so difficult just to wash the dishes, just to clean up our room, just to sit? And when we are hungry just to eat, when we are tired just to rest?

Why is that so difficult, just to practice the Way? Without reason, without knowing why, we practice *anuttara samyak sambodhi*, supreme awakening, supreme wisdom, the ultimate. Why do we sit? I don't know; we just do it, realizing the Bodhisattva Vow: we practice for the sake of liberating all beings.

There is no barrier. From the absolute point of view, there is absolutely nothing to pass through. The idea of going through something is all a hoax started by the Buddha. Blame him and all the masters who have carried it on after him. There is nothing stopping us from being our true selves. When we see this clearly, then what arises spontaneously is the Bodhisattva Vow. Since there is nothing to do, since there is no place to go, since there is nothing to gain—and yet everybody is looking for something, dissatisfied, suffering because they think there is something to get—then what comes up is a great compassion for others. We want to do something to help people realize what we have realized.

If we see somebody knocking his head against the wall constantly, then eventually, no matter how stubborn we are, we will go over and say: "Wait a minute, why don't you stop? This is not doing you any good." Some of us may not do that at first. We will just let people keep banging their heads against the brick wall. We have no compassion. But when we see people go on suffering, seeking, searching vainly in this dream, eventually it has to touch our hearts, raise the heart mind, arouse our compassion; and then we want to do something. That very compassion becomes the inspiration of Zen.

10 *Timeless Self-Essence*

If the eye never sleeps,
all dreams will naturally cease.
If the mind makes no discriminations,
the ten thousand things
are as they are, of single essence.
To understand the mystery of this One-essence
is to be released from all entanglements.
When all things are seen equally
the timeless Self-essence is reached.
No comparisons or analogies are possible
in this causeless, relationless state.

If the eye never sleeps,
all dreams will naturally cease.

What is the eye that never sleeps? One eye, two eyes, single eye, Zen eye: so many names for *prajna*. If *prajna* is awakened, all dreams naturally cease, all delusions and fantasies naturally come to an end. As we sit building up the power of concentration, or *joriki*, like inflating a balloon in our abdomen, we reach some equanimity, a certain stability. But as soon as we stop sitting, this power seeps away like air from a leaky balloon and we lose it. We have to keep sitting regularly to maintain the *joriki* in the lower abdomen. Then we have the stability and equanimity to handle situations in our lives more effectively.

When the power of *samadhi* is strong enough and we become really stable, when we have completely settled down in breath, body, and mind, then any chance event—hearing a bird chirping, seeing a sunset or a flower, looking into another's eyes, stubbing a toe, or getting whacked on the back by a stick—anything can open our eye when we are ready. Once the eye of *prajna* is completely open, it can never shut again. But until that happens, its tendency is to close, like the shutter of a camera lens. When it opens a little, we have a small experience, a *kensho* or glimpse into our nature, into the essence of mind, the essential aspect of the self. Then we see all dharmas as One, all things as one body; we realize the interdependence of all things.

If I get angry, it affects you. If you act lovingly, it affects me; even those as far away as the Soviet Union experience the vibrations. Whether they are aware of it or not, it is true. It is like a bowl of jelly: push or pull a little bit in one spot and everything in the bowl shakes. Sometimes we call this single essence *emptiness*, but it is not mere nothingness. When you really see it, you realize it is full, complete, whole. Emptiness is not substantial and yet not vacuous either.

Sometimes I use the analogy of snow. When the whole land is covered with snow, we can make all different kinds of snow statues: a mailman, a policewoman, a Santa Claus, a child, a dog, a cat, a killer, a Joan of Arc, and so on. These various forms appear different in shape and size, yet they are of a single essence: snow. To realize this One-essence is to free yourself. Free yourself from what? First of all, from having to seek after anything. If we are all made of the same essence, if everything arises from a single source, then everything is nothing but this one essence, through and through. The Sixth Patriarch called it "essence of Mind." Others call it "essential nature." Here the Third Patriarch calls it "timeless Self-essence." Bankei called it "unborn Buddha-mind." They all refer to the same thing: Buddha-nature, true self.

This essence is not born and can never die. It exists eternally. Some call it energy; others call it spirit. But what is it? No one knows. Any concept we have of what it is can only be an analogy, like snow. Buddha used an analogy also. Imagine the whole world were made of gold, he said, appearing in different forms, different shapes, different sizes, but each a form of gold. That is what you are, that is what everything is, pure gold. That is Buddha-nature.

When you really look into your own mind, you realize Mind is Buddha. Up until that point you think there cannot be Buddha-nature, or at least you doubt its existence. I ask you, "Who hears the sounds?" You look into your mind and you find nothing. But it is not nothing: nothing cannot hear. Try it sometime: ask empty space to hear sounds. Empty space cannot hear, cannot see, cannot think, cannot move. Mind thinks, sees, moves, hears.

But when I say *Mind*, I do not mean the thinking or conceptualizing that we normally associate with this word. When we go beyond dualistic or discriminating thinking, conceptual thought, what do we find? We find a space or gap between thoughts. We think nothing is there, but it is not nothing; it is Mind-essence. But if we think this essence is something that we can see, feel, grab hold of, we are wrong. Because everything is of that essence, it would be like trying to see our own eyes with our eyes or grasp our own hand with the same hand. We cannot do it. And yet, through our realization, we know there is the source, there is Buddha-nature, there is a true self—and we are it.

Your true self, your true identity, is not what we usually think, a tiny, limited individual: struggling, alienated, lonely, confused, scared, everything too much for us. Once we let go of the hold we have on the mind and the body, we merge with our true selves. But the word *merge* is inaccurate, because there was never anything keeping us separate and apart except our own dualistic thinking.

That is what *shikantaza* is, just sitting as one with all things at all times, not creating any kind of boundary or barrier or definition to separate ourselves. That is what koans are, too. To study koans is to question: what is Mind, what is *mu*, what is the source, what is Buddha, what is my original face?—all the same question. They all ask us to look into the mind, not to seek outside ourselves, not to seek in the future, but right now. These questions provoke us to see that our true nature is the Buddha-dharma, is the realization of the Way. As we are this very moment, as this very body and mind, we are the essence, which is manifesting itself all the time as me, as you, as everyone, as everything. Pure gold; pure snow. That is what is meant by true equality: we are all pure gold, all the same snow, all absolutely equal. We are all made out of the same essence, the same spirit, the same energy.

But we should not get stuck there. Mailman is still mailman; policewoman is still policewoman. Dog is dog; cat is cat. Child is child; parent is parent. Student is student; teacher is teacher. Man is man and woman is woman. When you finally realize your essential nature, you are complete. Male is already female; female is already male. It is already perfectly balanced. That is why, when men practice, the feminine side, the yin aspect, manifests. The more open, sensitive, aware, receptive side begins to come out. And the same with women: the yang aspect—the powerful, strong, assertive part—manifests in practice. You do not need to try to do anything about it, just accept it. Do not reject it, repress it, or disown it.

In our society, women tend to be repressed; but as they sit, they find down in the *hara*, in their bellies, infinite power. In fact, it is easy to get scared just by tapping into it a little bit. We do not know what to do with all that power. We think we cannot handle it, it might blow us apart, so we suppress it again. It takes time to have enough faith in ourselves to know that we can handle our full power, our true strength, and to allow it to come out. But the worst thing we can do is to hold back our power or try to cut down someone else's strength. When we attempt to sit on the energy, it is like sitting on a volcano. Go ahead and try— you won't succeed for long.

The same thing happens with the mind. When you try to control your mind too much and restrict it, it goes wild, like a wild horse or a crazy jumping monkey. Just let the thoughts arise when they arise, for it is going against the natural functioning of the mind to try to prevent them from arising. Still, you can cut off the thinking process by concentrating your attention in your lower belly. When you do that, what you find is tremendous energy beginning to flow. Just allow it to flow without trying to control it. Let thoughts come. What is wrong with thoughts?

When you are creating the space for all these thoughts to come up and at the same time remaining concentrated and focused, you won't be thinking dualistically. And what really happens the moment you say, "OK, thoughts, come up, I welcome you!" Suddenly there are no thoughts! What is happening? "Come on, thoughts, where are you?" Except for an occasional blip, they stop arising. Dogen Zenji said it a different way: "Drop body and mind. Let go of the mind and body." But don't worry: if somebody calls your name, you will be right there!

It is interesting to see what happens when we do not want to become unconscious and we are striving to stay conscious. We keep going to sleep anyway. The reason is simple: it is beyond our ability to put out the energy it takes to remain conscious all the time. We are bound to lose it, to start going to sleep, so we are constantly fighting unconsciousness. If instead we say, "OK, I'll let myself go unconscious," then we do not. In fact, we find it is impossible to go unconscious if we tell ourselves it is OK to do it. Maybe one moment we may be unconscious, but the next moment we are conscious again. We find that we keep returning to consciousness spontaneously, because we are not fighting anything, not exhausting ourselves by resisting sleep.

Clarity works the same way. We want so much to be clear. What for? What is wrong with confusion? Why do we have such a strong preference? What is so wonderful about clarity? We do not want to suffer and we think clarity will take away our suffering, so we cling to clarity in order to avoid suffering. Then that clinging becomes our problem, a new cause of suffering. What if you were really free and did not care anymore?

One time in *daisan* I asked someone how he was doing. "Not good. I am confused and angry." If you have been following what I am saying, you know immediately what was wrong. What was this person trying to accomplish? To drive away confusion and anger! Naturally he got confused and angry. I told him to sit up straight and be confused and angry. Two minutes later I asked, "What are you experiencing now?" "Clarity and peace," he said. "What happened to the confusion and anger?" "I don't know, I can't find them anymore."

It is a simple fact: whatever you resist will persist. If you are resisting suffering, you suffer more. If you are resisting confusion, you remain confused. If you are looking for peace, you find yourself constantly disturbed. If you are seeking after clarity, you are in a muddle. If you do not want to be angry, you are going to walk around angry. If you do not mind being angry, you will never be bothered about anger, because you will not be holding on to it. Having no opinion for or against, just being open to whatever comes, you are free.

> *If the mind makes no discriminations,*
> *the ten thousand things*
> *are as they are, of single essence.*

Do not prefer clarity over confusion, peace over conflict. Do not prefer pleasure over pain, happiness over unhappiness. Did you ever notice that people who want the most to be happy are always the most unhappy? They always say, "I want to be happy, but I never am." The people who do not care about happiness, who just work hard and do what they need to do, always seem to be happy. It is the same thing with people who want to be at peace. More than anything they want peace of mind, but their minds are always in conflict. They keep seeking greater peace and getting more conflict. Do not hold on to these discriminations and distinctions.

"The ten thousand things are as they are" refers to all things. A tree is a tree. A mountain is a mountain; a river is a river. Rivers flow; mountains do not. Dogs barks; cats meow. Did you ever see a barking cat or a meowing dog? When you are sitting and you hear a bark, you know it is a dog barking. That is what we call discriminating wisdom, the wisdom to know a dog from a cat. Can you tell a man from a woman? Then you have discriminating wisdom already! But as soon as we hold on to the idea that one is good and one is bad, something is right and something is wrong, right there it becomes discriminating delusion. When the subtlest notion of right or wrong appears, then we are lost in confusion.

> *To understand the mystery of this One-essence*
> *is to be released from all entanglements.*

This One-essence is a mystery. Everyone, everything is One-essence, yet what is it? No one can grasp it. You can live it: you can eat it, you can breathe it, you can be it; but you can never know it. Everything you can see is One-essence, but you can never see it. Everything you can hear is the One-essence, but you can never hear it. Every sound you hear is nothing but that One-essence, nothing but Buddhadharma. Every sound! That is why all sounds enlighten you. As Dogen Zenji said, "Be enlightened by the ten thousand things." Every sound you hear, everything you see, wakes you up, but you can never know the essence. You can only be it, for it is your life. The easiest thing in the world is to be it, since you cannot be anything but it. The most difficult, the really impossible thing is to grasp it.

> *When all things are seen equally*
> *the timeless Self-essence is reached.*

When you realize the Oneness, when you see the equality of all things, everything is just the One. When Enyadatta discovered her head, she exclaimed, "Ah, I have found my head at last! How wonderful! How extraordinary!" Then she realized that everybody has a head. What is so extraordinary about having a head? What is so extraordinary about being a Buddha? Everyone is Buddha. Everyone has Buddha-nature. Everything is Buddha. A barking dog is Buddha, a flower is a Buddha, even a piece of toilet paper is a Buddha.

What is so special? We are all just ordinary. But someone who is completely ordinary, that is an extraordinary person! It is said that when an ordinary person becomes enlightened, he or she becomes a sage; when a sage becomes enlightened, he or she becomes an ordinary person. First, all of us ordinary people must become enlightened, must become sages, must realize our timeless Self-essence—the unborn, undying, eternal self: no outside, no inside, no beginning, no end; our true nature that always has been and always will be. Then we must become ordinary, nothing special.

No comparisons or analogies are possible
in this causeless, relationless state.

You cannot compare it to anything because only the One-essence is, only Buddha-nature is. As soon as you start comparing, you have already split in two, fragmented yourself. "Causeless, relationless state" means in the absolute there is no cause and effect, no karma. How do we go beyond karma? When we drop mind and body, we become one with karma, we are just our karma, we live it from moment to moment. We have gone beyond. In that state there is no karma. That state is just karma.

No relationships! As soon as we have relationship, we are already split, already in duality. The relationless state, that is true communion: to be in unity, without boundary, without any barrier, without defenses. Some come into interview with all kinds of defenses up—to protect from what? Who is going to hurt you? Who is going to take advantage of you? If there are two in the room, certainly it is possible. If there is only one, it is impossible. From whom are we protecting ourselves?

Wouldn't it be wonderful to have no fear? That is the greatest gift: no fear! When you truly realize what *it* is, then there is no fear, nothing to hurt you, nothing to destroy you. Nothing can take your life, because your life is unborn, therefore undying. All the rest is a dream.

11 *Movement and Stillness Disappear*

Consider motion in stillness
and stillness in motion,
both movement and stillness disappear.
When such dualities cease to exist
Oneness itself cannot exist.
To this ultimate finality
no law or description applies.

For the unified mind in accord with the Way
all self-centered striving ceases.
Doubts and irresolutions vanish
and life in true faith is possible.
With a single stroke we are freed from bondage;
nothing clings to us and we hold to nothing.
All is empty, clear, self-illuminating,
with no exertion of the mind's power.
Here thought, feeling, knowledge, and imagination
      are of no value.
In this world of Suchness
there is neither self nor other-than-self.

Consider motion in stillness
and stillness in motion,
both movement and stillness disappear.

When we are sitting strongly in zazen, in that stillness, in that very motionlessness, there is complete and perfect motion. Mae-zumi Roshi makes an analogy with a child's toy top. When you spin the top just right and it stays upright in one spot, not meandering around but in perfect balance, then there is a stillness, as if it were not moving at all, and it appears to lose its form. When the top is off balance, then it wobbles all over and looks very solid. Spinning well, it becomes formless; it even begins to appear transparent.

That is just how our zazen is. When we sit well, the flow of energy is more balanced. That energy which is flowing throughout the body allows us to become aware of our transparent and formless nature, to experience our form, this very body, as empty. That is what *shikantaza* really is. When you are sitting zazen and ask yourself what true emptiness is, you realize immediately: just *this*! This very posture, the body-mind itself, is transparent, empty, formless, no-self.

When we go into any activity, work or play, if we really put ourselves into it completely, not holding back even one percent, doing it with complete faith and determination and throwing ourselves into it, then we disappear. Then in our very movement there is stillness, peace of mind. Yet it is that very disappearing, that mini-death experience, which we fear. And the fear is exactly what keeps us from putting ourselves totally into anything we do. Maybe we put 99 percent or even 99.9 percent, but we will not go the whole way; we hold back. Always there is resistance to doing it completely. Beneath any reason that we give is fear, fear of dying or disappearing in that activity. When we are totally engaged, we are completely still within the activity. There is complete silence and in that silence there is no self, no *I*. That is why in all religions throughout the ages mystics have sought after inner silence, the still point. In that very quietness there is no thought. When there is no thought, then there is no *me*, no self.

Dogen Zenji entitled the first fascicle of his *Shobogenzo* "Genjo Koan," absolute reality, the true koan in realization. That is just what the Third Patriarch is referring to here. In all activity, when there is true stillness, it is the koan of reality, the reality itself in manifestation. What is that koan in realization? Nothing but you, every moment of your life. When you are sitting, true self is just sitting; when you are moving, true self is just moving; when you are bowing, true self is just bowing.

We have the koan: "Be an immovable tree in a heavy wind." Unmoving, yes, but if you are rigid and inflexible in a hurricane, you will snap or be uprooted. In so many of our professions we become rigid, especially the ones based primarily on intellect, knowledge, stored-up information, like the legal field. It is easy to get very rigid when you have to take a position. And when you rely on the intellect, you have to be especially careful not to get fixated.

Taking a fixed position is the complete opposite of our practice. Our practice is to be an immovable tree in a heavy wind, meaning to be very deeply rooted. Rooted in what? In the Buddhadharma, in zazen; rooted in the core of the earth, the very center, and yet able to bend with the wind, flow with the current; not to stand proud and straight and rigid against it, but to be flexible. We do not have to argue a position unless that is our job. We do not have to be unbending or unyielding nor do we have to apologize constantly for our position, either. If we believe we are right, we can go ahead, but we must also be willing to see the other side constantly.

Koan study is about being able to let go of one position and move around to see the koan from different perspectives. Always there are different perspectives: the relative and the absolute, mine and yours, and so on. If sometimes the teacher says *no* to your presentation of a koan and you are sure you are right, maybe you are correct from the absolute side but wrong from the relative side, or vice versa. Anytime you get stuck on your understanding, on your rightness, you are wrong.

For example, "What is the source of *mu?*" Some of you come in and say, "*I* am the source of *mu.*" No! You are sticking to one side. You have to be willing to drop that, let it go, and look at the koan again from another perspective. As long as you stick to your old perspective, you can never go through it. A koan like that one is exactly what I was talking about earlier. It takes a 100 percent effort. An effort of 99.999 percent will not really do it, though the teacher can pass you any time. The difference between your first glimpse of that koan, which might be called an opening or *kensho*, and really seeing it with absolute certainty, knowing without any doubt what it is, that can be the difference between hell and nirvana, between heaven and earth.

What makes that difference is knowing in your heart that you have given everything. You have completely thrown yourself into the koan, become the koan, become utterly one with the koan and sought the answer from within the koan, from being that source. Then you know that all striving and all seeking are absolutely in vain. No amount of effort can possibly grasp the ungraspable, realize the unrealizable.

What is the difference between our knowing now and someone like Bodhidharma's? When he was 112 years old and Emperor Wu asked, "Who are you?" he replied "I know *not!*" There is a big difference between that powerful statement of truth and our uncertain, "Oh . . . I don't know . . . "—the difference between a sage and a nerd. We are the nerds because we are not ready to throw ourselves completely into our practice.

Why do we resist, hold back? Out of fear, of course. But if you want to be free of fear, liberated, you have to know your own mind. And to know your own mind you have to look into it and find out who you are. Even if I were to tell you from the beginning, that would not help. You must realize for yourself that you are *it*. If we call that absolute "God," then be God! If we call it Christ, just be Christ! But we are taught in our society that you cannot be or even say such things. What happens in this society when we say, "I am Christ"? Off to the insane asylum!

Just recently I was on a panel with a Catholic monk, an Episcopal priest, and some psychiatrists addressing four hundred and fifty people in the helping professions. At one point I said, "I am Jesus Christ! I am God!" and I was waiting for the lynch mob. Yet somehow they seemed to appreciate it, because all of us know in our hearts that it is the truth: "I am the Way; I am the Truth!" Christ said it and he was crucified. But in Zen, that is what we have to be willing to realize and to admit, dropping all the baloney we have been taught, all our conditioning about what is right and wrong.

When I first started this practice, I realized right away that you can think this, but you cannot say it unless you go crazy or get into a profession where your craziness is accepted. Maybe Zen monks have to be crazy. Buddha said it this way: "Above the heavens and below the heavens, I alone am the Revered One!" I am the Buddha! Why is it so difficult for us really to admit to it? We think that it shows a big ego: "I can't say that until I drop my ego." But if your ego becomes that big, it has no outside; it has to include everybody, everything. It is a misconception to think we can get rid of the ego or make it smaller. When the ego includes everything, it ceases to be ego. Then we can see that there is no ego.

What did the Buddha realize? There is no ego, no individual self. For him, the boundary dissolved, like a bubble bursting on the surface of the water. When there is a bubble, there is an individual. When the bubble breaks, there is just the water. When that boundary disappears, you are one with the cosmic ocean. Denying the ego does not work. Admit the truth! Then what is God? When you really become one with it, even that disappears. You need not hold on to such concepts.

> *When such dualities cease to exist*
> *Oneness itself cannot exist.*

Even Oneness can become a concept. We have a saying: "The many become the One." Many dharmas, all things, become One. This One becomes zero and zero becomes all things. When we truly become one with *mu*, one with any single thing, even one task, we become zero, nothing. The no-self is mountains, trees, rocks, grass, and stars—everything everywhere—no boundary, no barrier, no wall.

> *To this ultimate finality*
> *no law or description applies.*

In this ultimate reality, anything we think or say about it fails to describe it. It remains forever unnameable. When you have the experience and you try to express ultimate reality, somehow it never comes out quite right. We can point to it, talk about it, the words themselves are nothing but it, and yet the words cannot describe it. Despite this, the hunger always comes up to express it. In the Zen tradition, you are not seeing it clearly until you can express the inexpressible. The first thing in koan study is to realize the Oneness, then to realize the function of this undifferentiated Oneness, then finally to realize how to express the inexpressible.

For the unified mind in accord with the Way
all self-centered striving ceases.

When you have given 100 percent and you see without a shadow of a doubt the absolute absurdity of such striving, when you have worn out this constantly seeking mind, when you have exhausted yourself like Enyadatta fighting against the ropes in her desperation to find her head, and you finally come to rest, then all striving ceases. But somehow we do it partially and so do not come to full realization right away. We do it 99 percent and feel at peace for a while, thinking we have attained something, then doubt arises once more. Somehow we are not satisfied, so again we go through the search.

The tendency is not to want to admit that there is still doubt, but to hold on to the idea: "I have done it, I have realized it." If the teacher tells us it is just an illusion, we want to say "horseshit" to the teacher. We do not want to admit that our realization is incomplete. Doubt builds and builds, until finally it becomes so great, so painful, so discouraging, that, stubborn and hopeless as we are, we have no choice: we have to admit to ourselves that we have not realized anything. Of course, when we do admit that, we are forced to face doubt in our teacher, the practice, and the Way.

Up to now, we have been passing koan after koan, perhaps we have even finished with koan study. How can we still not be satisfied? How can there still be doubt? How can something in us still be hungry for the truth? Now we must be willing to experience total doubt: doubt in the Way, doubt in our teacher, doubt in our experiences, doubt in ourselves, doubt in the Buddha, doubt in all the Patriarchs, and be willing to say, "What the hell does the Buddha know anyway? How do I know he realized anything? And all those masters, who the hell were they? For all I know they could have been just as dumb as me. And my teacher? He is nothing special either."

In order to be able to face such extreme doubt, we have got to have a foundation of true faith. Otherwise we simply will not allow ourselves to doubt like that, to go through that kind of pain, anguish, and desperation, having faith in nothing. But if it is faith in something, it is not true faith. We can call it faith in ourselves, but who are we? We don't know, yet the faith is there, a trust in our true selves, not in our egos. There must be a willingness to face the fear, to be willing to make the great leap from the hundred-foot pole again and again, and then, once and for all, really to die to the self and stand completely alone without any support or approval, without leaning on anyone or anything—free of all principles, free of the teacher, free of everything. Always we have been looking for approval from the teacher, but the final approval has to come from ourselves. Then the teacher can confirm it.

In the Rinzai tradition, it is said that when there is great doubt, there is great enlightenment; mediocre doubt, mediocre realization; small doubt, small realization. We go through numerous doubts and numerous openings, *kenshos*, until finally there is enough stability, enough foundation of trust and faith to go through the last barrier, the final gate. Of course, even after that we can get stuck in the very realization of nothing to attain. From the beginning, what have we been lacking, what has been in excess? Absolutely nothing! From the beginning, everything is perfect and complete as is. So, why make any effort? Why strive? Why seek? We can get attached to the experience of this nothing, and then we have to drop that, too.

Doubts and irresolutions vanish
and life in true faith is possible.

After we have gone through such an experience, it is possible to live in true faith. Then there is nothing to prove, no place to go, nothing to do. As Rinzai said, there is just being your ordinary self, with nothing further to attain; riding home on the back of the ox playing your flute or sitting in your garden after the ox has gone. But still there is further to go.

With a single stroke we are freed from bondage;
nothing clings to us and we hold to nothing.

When you go through that great doubt, that great fear, you realize not that you are now free, but rather that you have *always* been free, you have never been bound or fettered in any way. There has never been any barrier; that is all delusion, a dream. You have never been two, separated, dual; all that was created in the mind. Then you are really, truly free. Of course, when we get attached to that liberation, then the very liberation itself becomes a bondage. You have to let go even of freedom and be willing to be unfree. You must be free enough to be unfree, to go back into the marketplace with a heavy load, to become a deluded Bodhisattva. Our ordinary mind cannot grasp this.

How can we be free enough to be sick, with all sentient beings? Free enough to be fettered in everything? To be willing to exist in the muddiest of mud, because that is where all sentient beings reside? And to be no better, no different, nobody special? Really to be just ordinary? Who would allow such a thing? Who is willing to go to the depths of hell, to put in so much effort, so much striving, just to be completely ordinary? But if we resist this—and we *all* resist it—we stay attached.

All is empty, clear, self-illuminating,
with no exertion of the mind's power.

No mental effort, no struggle to control one's self or to dominate others; just to let be, let go, drop all exertion: that is true *shikantaza.* When there is no longer any trying or any clinging—that is complete stillness in motion and complete motion in stillness. When you sit like that, the energy just flows; it doesn't stop anywhere and is not limited to any one area.

Here thought, feeling, knowledge, and imagination
are of no value.

Always we have held on to something: the importance of our thoughts, the importance of our feelings, the importance of our knowledge and imagination. Now we go beyond all such things.

> *In this world of Suchness*
> *there is neither self nor other-than-self.*

No "me," no "you"—no Oneness, either. Just eating. Just resting. Just sitting. Just picking one's nose. Not looking for anything.

12 *Not Two*

To come directly into harmony with this reality
just simply say when doubt arises, "Not two."
In this "not two" nothing is separate,
nothing is excluded.
No matter when or where,
enlightenment means entering this truth.
And this truth is beyond extension or
   diminution in time or space;
in it a single thought is ten thousand years.

To come directly into harmony with this reality
just simply say when doubt arises, "Not two."

If I were asked what our practice is all about, I would have to
say to be one—not split, not dual. The aim of koan study is
learning how to be one with each koan. We have a whole series
of koans called *hosshin*, Dharma body or Dharma mind koans.
Mind and body in this case mean the same thing: one body, like
mu or one's face before one's parents were born or the sound of
one hand. All these are called *dharmakaya hosshin* koans. The
whole point is just to be it.

If your koan is *mu*, just be *mu*: not two, not *mu* separated
from the one working on *mu*. In *daisan* sometimes people say,
"My name is such-and-such and my koan is *mu*." Every time I
hear that, I want to say, "My name is *mu* and I am working on
Genpo!" Your real name is *mu* and you are working on whoever
you think you are. As Dogen Zenji said, "To study the Buddha
Way is to study the self," to work on one's self.

What are all these sutras, or scriptures, we study? Hannyatara, Bodhidharma's teacher, was asked to say grace at a dinner party given by Bodhidharma's father, who was the ruler of India. Just as in the West, at big ceremonial dinners the priest or minister with the most seniority says the grace. Hannyatara was the Twenty-seventh Patriarch and also the king's and Bodhidharma's teacher, so he was asked. Hannyatara said, "When I breathe in I revolve the ten thousand sutras and when I breathe out I revolve the ten thousand sutras." Every time you inhale and exhale you are expounding the sutra. Every time you hear, you hear the sutra. Every time you speak, the sutra is speaking. Everything you see is the sutra. The one seeing is nothing but the sutra, this Dharma. Your life, that is the sutra. Your life, that is the Dharma.

How can it be two? How can it be separate from your life? If you expect someday you are going to realize what the Dharma is, someday you are going to find the Dharma, that is insanity. It is like thinking some day you are going to find your head, that it can be lost. The very thought that something has been lost, that the Dharma is missing or that truth is absent, not yet realized, that is the insanity! People come in to *daisan* and say things like, "I haven't realized *it* yet. Ten years I have been studying and I haven't realized anything yet." You should laugh when you see the absurdity of such statements. Already you are free. How can a Buddha become a Buddha? If Buddha becomes Buddha, then Buddha is a freak, a two-headed monster!

It is so simple: the telephone rings—why do we answer it? The bell sounds—why do we put on our robes and come to sit? Someone came to *daisan* and said, "Sometimes I wonder why I am here, why I am sitting." That is beautiful: to wonder why we are sitting and why we are practicing and yet to stay here and do this crazy practice. To get up at four-thirty A.M. and sit for ten hours a day, facing a stupid wall! How do we explain that to anybody? Even dumber than doing it is trying to explain it to someone. Who is going to understand? The truth is, we don't know anyway. When we examine it closely, we don't know. What keeps us in this practice year after year? Not really knowing, we just do it.

This is actually the meaning of the title, *Hsin hsin ming*: faith in mind, mind faith, or mind truth. This is real faith: not knowing why, just to do it. The same applies to koan study. For instance, "What is Zen? The cow shitting in the field." To be one with this koan, just to be the koan takes tremendous faith and lack of self-consciousness. If you hold on to self, you cannot be one with the koan, you will hold back. And always, somehow, that is our problem, too self-conscious, restrained, inhibited. Maybe it is how we are raised: "Don't do that, somebody might object," or, "Don't do that, people are watching." Then always we are looking over our shoulders for someone to be looking and criticizing us. We become more and more self-conscious and that self-consciousness is exactly what impedes us, hinders us from being free, from being ourselves. If you can answer the koan, "What is Zen? Cow shitting in the field," you shouldn't have any problem.

Already you have tasted two glasses of champagne and you say your mouth is not yet moistened? That is true arrogance, greed. Doesn't greed stem from arrogance, from egoism, thinking that we exist separate and apart from everybody else? Isn't it arrogant and greedy to think we are not enlightened, we haven't realized enough yet? Have you ever thought about it that way? Usually we think the opposite: "It would be arrogant to think I've realized *it*, to admit to it, to admit the Truth."

It is not two. And if *it* is not two, then who is left to know? And to know what? Aren't two required to know something, the knower and the known? Then knowing something is already moving apart from Truth, separating yourself from the Way. As soon as you seek after *it*, try to know *it*, you have already gone astray. To try to know *it* is arrogance; to try to understand *it* is our conceited mind.

When we try so hard to know and finally we realize: "I don't know and *it* cannot be known . . . *it* is ungraspable and unattainable . . . *it* is just *this*," doesn't that truly humble us? So humiliating, trying for five, ten, fifteen, even twenty years, like an idiot, and failing completely! Isn't that humiliation enough?

In our practice, really to fail, once and for all, to fail absolutely and completely: that is *it*.

Of course, what do we do? We come to each retreat to win, to make it through. I don't know how many times I have said to myself: "I made it through another one." If you can say, "I made it!" you lost. You won the battle and lost the war. If you can say once and for all, "I didn't make it; this one I didn't survive, I completely failed; this one killed me," then you got it! Really fail, really lose: that is winning. As Koryu Roshi, one of Maezumi Roshi's teachers, always said, "Once and for all, die on your cushion!" Once you really die the Great Death, you cannot die ever again. Life becomes eternal.

> *In this "not two" nothing is separate,*
> *nothing is excluded.*

That is *shikantaza*. That is *mu*. That is koan. That is zazen. Normally we set up all kinds of walls and barriers simply by defining ourselves. As soon as we define something, we set up criteria about it, contrast it with other things. Once it is defined, we can study it, understand it. Now we feel more comfortable because we can comprehend it. But ultimately there is nothing to define, only no-self: vast space.

Ordinarily we define ourselves in limiting ways: I am a man or a woman; I am uneducated or highly educated; I am arrogant or humble, brilliant or stupid, old or young, deluded or awakened. All just concepts! Why are we afraid to throw out all definitions, all concepts, all ideas? Who or what would we be then? How would we relate? How would we function, not knowing? How could we go to work if we didn't know who we were?

This brings us back to faith. If you really trust and have faith, you can live without such definitions and then you are not limited. Then you are the boundless, infinite nothing. But who wants to be nothing? Because we don't want to be nothing, we cannot be infinite. So we settle for being just a little something, not much. Just throw it out! Then you can receive all, be all. When you really empty yourself of the self, then you are the mountains, the rivers, the earth—everything. You are all things.

Only then does true compassion arise. Then you cannot turn your back on another, because that other is not separate from yourself. Then it is hard to be greedy for one's self. Of course you can still be greedy for the whole, for the Dharma, for the Truth, for people to awaken. All the time Maezumi Roshi used to say: "I want you to be really greedy; you are not greedy enough!" and "I don't want you to be desireless. Have big desire, great desire!" What are the Four Vows after all? Nothing but huge desire: to liberate all sentient beings, to accomplish the Way!

> *No matter when or where,*
> *enlightenment means entering this truth.*

There is the story about when Hui-neng, who later became the Sixth Patriarch, went to visit the Fifth Patriarch. Here was Hui-neng, a young, self-confident whipper-snapper, filled with all kinds of wisdom. Testing him, the Fifth Patriarch said, "In southern China where you come from, I hear there is no Buddhadharma!" Hui-neng replied, "The Buddhadharma knows no north, south, east, or west." Whatever the generation, whatever the age, whatever the culture, whatever the country, the Truth is universal. No matter what our upbringing, our training, our conditioning, no matter even (believe it or not) how badly we have been mistreated by our parents, still we are capable of realizing this Truth. Even you, in this very lifetime.

Some of you think, "I will never do it in one lifetime; it will take me lifetime after lifetime!" But at any moment it is only an instant away. You can be going in completely the wrong direction, then turn around and there it is. It is never further away than this moment, than this ground under your feet. It is right in front of your nose. You can be a completely deluded know-it-all and, in the very next instant, a Buddha!

That is what is meant by the sudden school. Tokusan before his enlightenment was such a renowned authority on the *Diamond Sutra* that people called him "Diamond teacher." He believed it took lifetimes to become a Buddha and all those who taught that you could realize enlightenment in one instant were heretics. He went on a journey to challenge them all and was defeated by Master Ryutan. In the instant when the master blew out a candle in the darkness, Tokusan had a sudden realization. Then he burned all his sutras.

Regardless of preconceptions, there is not one individual who is incapable of suddenly awakening. It depends only on how desperately you want it, how determined you are. With great determination you can do it; with minimum determination you cannot. The desperate fool will do it, the arrogant phony will not. The one who keeps it all together, who keeps up a facade, a pretense of equanimity, the one who is unwilling to let go completely, will not. The one who is willing to give up, to let go of body and mind, will realize; the one who is holding on cannot. Just let it all go.

> *And this truth is beyond extension or*
> *diminution in time or space;*
> *in it a single thought is ten thousand years.*

We cannot add to this Truth and we cannot take anything away from it. It is beyond knowing and beyond not-knowing. It is beyond this and that; beyond past and future, here and now. It is not in some other place and it is not here, either. If you know it, you have already missed it. If you don't know it, you never will. And yet, each of us is freely using it all the time. That means each one of us is already free. The Truth is functioning right now; but as soon as you try to grasp it, it eludes you. If you turn away from it, you will never get it. What should you do? Just be it!

13 *Empty Infinity*

> Emptiness here, Emptiness there,
> but the infinite universe stands
> always before your eyes.
> Infinitely large and infinitely small;
> no difference, for definitions have vanished
> and no boundaries are seen.
> So too with Being and non-Being.
> Don't waste time in doubts and arguments
> that have nothing to do with this.

> *Emptiness here, Emptiness there,*
> *but the infinite universe stands*
> *always before your eyes.*

This reminds me of Rinzai's four propositions. The first is that all dharmas are empty. It is rather easy to get a glimpse of that: the world that we live in, everything, is empty. After I saw that clearly, then there was nothing left except the Dharma, except practice. The world, all that I was doing, all that I was seeking after, all my ambitions, desires, everything I wanted, was altogether empty and without purpose. The way we have been pursuing our lives, how we have been trained and conditioned to seek after all kinds of things: name, fame, fortune, position; it is all completely empty of meaning.

Rinzai's second proposition states that the self, this very body, is empty: no self-nature, no entity, only clear space. Nothing to cling to called *I* or *me*, so nobody to get upset; no one left to be angry or frightened. The second level is actually to realize that.

Then, third, is realizing that all together all dharmas and body and mind are empty. This is the very state we call the Great Death, *dai kensho*. And, simultaneously, fourth, when we die the Great Death, when we fully experience all dharmas and the self as empty, then we have what we call great rebirth or great liberation: new life, the life that is unborn and undying, complete freedom.

These four propositions expound just what the Third Patriarch is saying: "Emptiness here, Emptiness there" means self is empty and all dharmas are empty. And when the empty universe "stands always before your eyes," that is the great rebirth. Some of you come in to *daisan* and say, "Nothing exists." I ask you, "Show me this nothing." Just look around: people, carpet, altar, flower, trees, land; wherever you go, there is the infinite universe. This infinite universe, all things, everything you see, is nothingness; but you cannot separate the nothing from the something. Our minds are so crazy. We want to separate out the emptiness from the form, the formless from the form. Formlessness is form. Form is formlessness. All dharmas, all things, are empty. The infinite universe, all the planets, all the stars, all the cosmos, all empty, infinitely small, infinitesimally small. Zero!

That is the beautiful thing: whichever direction you go ends up the same way. If you expand your mind to include the whole universe, if you make it infinitely large, it has no outside, no boundary. It is limitless, boundless, infinite. That is zero; that is nothing. It has no inside, either; no self, no separate nature. Or go to the opposite extreme: concentrate your mind on one thing. Focus it down like a magnifying lens on a tiny point, a dot. Then reduce that one point down to nothing: you have before your eyes all things, an infinite universe, empty infinity.

That is our essential nature. Where does this essence abide? We say it is nonabiding, but where is this nonabiding place? All things, this form, this body. The infinite universe stands always before your eyes. Close your eyes: become nothing. Open your eyes: there is the universe. You cannot get rid of it. Sometimes we want to annihilate the universe; we hear of or experience emptiness and imagine we can eliminate everything.

Infinitely large and infinitely small;
no difference, for definitions have vanished
and no boundaries are seen.

That is what our sitting is about: to let go of all definitions. We are so busy defining: defining our selves, our positions, our work, our words. What are words? Words are the prison cell that we reside in. We say Zen is beyond words and letters, because we use words to imprison ourselves. Many koans give us precisely the opportunity to break free of the bondage of words.

We get stuck in a word or a phrase and then we are not free. For instance, "How would you eat food or drink tea without using your lips?" Would you try a straw? I think some of you might. I remember giving a koan I made up: "How do you get out of this room without using your hands?" Some of the attempts were wonderful: using feet, elbows, or even mouth, jumping up and grabbing on, trying to turn the door knob.

How we get stuck on words. Take the koan "Empty-handed and yet holding a stick," for example. How can we be empty and yet hold a stick? It is completely contradictory. What is our fear? If I don't have my universe clearly defined, then how do I relate to it? The word *relate* itself is the problem. I can only relate to something other than myself. Many koans hinge on this, like "What is the sound of one hand?" One of the testing questions asks, "How do you cut the one hand in two?" I am always afraid someone is going to present me some amputated fingers or come in and cut their hand in two. Then I would have to give it back to them and say, "No, Wrong."

Someone once said that the whole universe is nothing but one big sword, Manjushri's sword. Manjusri is the Bodhisattva of wisdom; his sword cuts through all delusion and brings enlightenment to all beings. But there was one person that Manjushri could never enlighten. Who was that? Do you think you are? No, it was Vimalakirti, a layman whose spiritual attainment was unsurpassed. Vimalakirti was sick and Buddha asked all his disciples to go see what was troubling him. All went, one after another, and had Dharma combat with Vimalakirti. When Manjushri asked Vimalakirti why he was ill, he replied, "All sentient beings are ill, therefore I am ill. My sickness will last as long as there is ignorance and self-clinging. As long as beings are sick, I myself will remain sick. When all beings are liberated from ignorance, then the Bodhisattva will be free of sickness. For Bodhisattvas treasure all beings like their own children. The Bodhisattva's sickness arises from great compassion."

We have to become healthy enough to fall ill. When we are still trying to be strong, defending ourselves, we can't let ourselves get sick. We force ourselves to stay well because we don't feel strong enough to be vulnerable; we can't allow ourselves to be weak. Vimalakirti, out of his great compassion, remained sick.

Kanzeon, or Kannon, the embodiment of compassion, is also like this. Because all sentient beings are deluded, Kanzeon remains deluded. Delusion is a concept; enlightenment is another concept. Healthy is a concept; sick is another concept. We seek after health and try to avoid sickness, seek after enlightenment and try to escape delusion. All are just concepts!

Without concepts we find ourselves unbounded, undefined; and our greatest fear is to live without boundaries, without definitions. Of course, when we have no boundaries, we are vulnerable. Everyone, everything can come in. There are no separations, no barriers to protect us. That is why we put up personal boundaries, to protect ourselves from people, from things, from disease, from accidents, and ultimately from death. First we define ourselves: *me* versus *you, me* against *not-me*. Then we fortify the boundary, making the wall bigger and stronger. Pretty soon we have a really thick wall around ourselves. We are completely protected from the *not-me*.

One day we turn around and we realize what we have done: we have imprisoned ourselves. We can keep the world out, but now we are stuck inside. Then we wonder, "How did I get here in this prison cell? Who did this to me? Who are the culprits?" We wonder why we cannot feel anything, cannot even see or smell or taste anything. The first time I realized this, I was amazed: I heard the universe for the first time. And the sounds! I had never known they were there, because I had put up a wall of fog between me and the world and I had been living in that pea soup, wallowing in it and muddling around in it, not really seeing or hearing anything.

Practice is how to break down that wall. First we try to charge into it, but we find it is like solid cement or iron. We have to bang into it over and over again until we finally realize how extremely thick the wall really is. Trying, trying, trying, but to no avail; we cannot seem to get anywhere. Finally, after trying so hard, we turn around and find we can step out of the very same doorway we entered. This is realizing we created the wall in our minds by defining and labeling ourselves. If we stop creating concepts of ourselves, then there is no such barrier. The wall from the beginning was unreal. That is what the name of the famous koan collection, *Mumonkan*, means: "gateless gate." There was never a wall, never any barrier, never anything to go through.

And yet in the beginning we have certain experiences of breaking through. Something drops away and there is a momentary sensation of freedom, peace, liberation. Of course, immediately we are looking for another breakthrough. Then we are on a roller coaster; we get really hooked. We try harder, and the harder we try, the more we find ourselves getting nowhere. Now we really believe there is something to break through. We remember the sense of freedom when we dropped off something and we want to repeat it, whether it was on top of a mountain, or sitting by a stream or by the ocean, or feeling a breeze, or whatever. So we try and try, fruitlessly, and one day, not trying, we just relax and it happens again. Then we want it to be permanent.

Do you see how greedy we are? We want that state to last forever, like John Lennon, who tried taking LSD constantly so that he never had to come down. Finally after several hundred acid trips he had to stop and where was he then? Right back in the prison, hundreds of drug trips later. It is a dualistic attitude, not liking it the way it is, not being satisfied with this crummy, deluded world. We always want more of something we have experienced. That is what is meant by having tasted three cups of the best wine and still our lips are not yet moistened.

One of Bodhidharma's four disciples, Emperor Wu's daughter, said: "Once I glimpsed it, I never looked back." In other words, "I never went after it again." Who is able to drop all seeking, all searching, *completely* like that? If you cannot drop it, then at least search totally. What happens when you do something completely? If you completely surrender to suffering, what happens to your suffering? It disappears. If you are angry and you are completely angry and don't hold any of it back, what happens to the anger? It just dissolves.

What happens, then, if you seek completely, one hundred percent? Seeking disappears, then you think you did something wrong: "I didn't try hard enough. Maybe next *sesshin* . . ." Key point: be one! "Not two" is an even better way of saying it. Whatever is going on, be one with it; don't be separate from it, don't split yourself in two.

We have a koan, "All dharmas are nothing but mind. In what place do you seek for the mind?" "Where is this mind? Where did it go? . . . It was here just a minute ago!" That is exactly what we do: we have a little taste, then we are immediately looking for it, earnestly searching to find it again, rather than just being one with our delusion, our suffering. Why do we make it so hard? Why do we always want it better?

> *So too with Being and non-Being.*
> *Don't waste time in doubts and arguments*
> *that have nothing to do with this.*

Being or nonbeing was an important question for me: "Do I exist or not?" Our rational minds, of course, see it as either/or: either we exist or we don't exist. Sitting long enough, we start to realize, "Maybe I don't exist." Then we look around, "But what is moving, what is hearing, what is seeing, what is walking around? Something must be doing all this. I have got to exist!" Yet in our glimpses, our little experiences, nothing exists. Nothing! Our logical minds simply cannot put the two together. Either we exist or we don't exist. We always want to figure it out, to understand, to know. Do we choose being or nonbeing? Coming or going? Life or death?

We think life and death are separate phenomena. We never think of life and death as the same; that would be illogical. Only one problem, one small problem: reality is not logical. Truth is not rational; only our minds are. We are so egotistical, so arrogant, that we want to make reality into a concept, reduce life to a logical idea. We spend all our time looking for some concept of Truth, but Truth is what is left when we drop all concepts. Then there is just scratching when it itches.

14 *To Live in This Faith*

One thing, all things:
move among and intermingle,
without distinction.
To live in this realization
is to be without anxiety about nonperfection.
To live in this faith is the road to nonduality,
because the nondual is one with the trusting mind.

Words!
The Way is beyond language,
for in it there is

> no yesterday
> no tomorrow
> no today.

One thing, all things:
move among and intermingle,
without distinction.

When we drop our dualistic, discriminating mind, when we drop boundaries and labels, then everything is as it is: changing constantly, moving, intermingling, inseparable! That is what we call in Buddhism Indra's net: everything interconnects with and reflects everything else.

To live in this realization
is to be without anxiety about nonperfection.

We get caught up in trying to be perfect. If we really have faith in our practice, we can throw ourselves completely into our zazen, not trying to become anything, obtain anything, or get rid of anything.

Sometimes we say this practice is all about going beyond suffering or freeing ourselves from misery. Perhaps that is why we are sitting, because our lives have been very dissatisfying, lonely, full of depression, anxiety, fears, and painful situations, and we want to get rid of all that. But the very desire to get rid of anything is wrong understanding. Why not appreciate these various conditions? What would life be without dull, boring, even painful things?

When we eat, sometimes we like to put some spice in our food. Like spice, these unpleasant conditions make life interesting. Sometimes we are upset, sometimes angry, sometimes elated, sometimes depressed. Why sit there despising and trying to avoid these various feelings? Invite them, welcome them, knowing that our practice is to experience everything fully, to be completely one with whatever arises.

Why be picking and choosing? Only good feelings, good thoughts should come up, only joy? Even if that were possible, such an attitude is shabby practice. Sit without holding preferences for or against anything, being open to whatever comes up. We have suppressed so much for so long, trying to stay in control, afraid we might even kill somebody, that we have become like walking volcanoes. Once we really open ourselves up, open our hearts, then whatever is ready to come up just comes up. Experiencing it completely, being one with it, everything is all right: we can relax and just let it release in its own way.

During my first year of practice, I lived alone in a cabin in the mountains for the whole year with only an occasional visitor. People used to ask if I was lonely, but I had been around people so much in my life that by then I was craving to be alone and really enjoyed it. But somehow in our society we are given the idea that we cannot enjoy being alone. At sundown, after a long sit, I would sip a little wine and just be with myself. It was a deeply pleasurable experience and the only time in my life I ever wrote poetry. Much anger came up for me, too. It was awful; I had to accept that it was my anger, nobody else's. But once accepted, that anger turned into positive energy, power for zazen. Our practice is to include all things, not to avoid or exclude anything. All-inclusive practice, that is what *shikantaza* means.

Give up trying to become perfect. Do you realize that what most people like best about you is your imperfections? When I was teaching school, I remember sometimes a whole classroom would be filled with angels, but I always seemed to get the devils. I admit it, I encouraged them. They were more interesting, much more colorful than the angels. My favorite students were the ones I had the most difficulty with. I still remember their names but not the names of the angels.

To be flawless is not to be perfect. If you are a perfect angel, you really stink. Maezumi Roshi said that if you strive to live by the precepts and you think you are really succeeding in maintaining them, then you are sick; right there you are actually breaking the precepts with your arrogance. If you think you are perfect, then already things are not OK.

Have faith and trust in what you are and do not sit to be perfect. Sit because that is your true nature, which is in realization when you sit; that is reason enough to do it. In other words, you don't sit to become an enlightened person, but rather, since you are already an awakened person, you sit.

But is it really enough just to sit? I am not saying we should not continue to clarify our understanding, but even the desire to clarify at some point will become a hindrance. So go one step beyond that: sit and just be one with the muddle. Don't try to get rid of confusion or delusion; don't try to understand or seek enlightenment.

Early in our zazen practice we think we have realized something and we know where we are going, but somehow as we progress we seem to know less and less. After a few years, as much as we really want to know, we don't seem to know much at all. Go beyond knowing and not knowing. Along the way there are points of not knowing and not even thinking that we know, and then there is that point of going beyond knowing and not knowing, when we know clearly that we do not know, cannot possibly know. When you know like that, you can really say "I know *not!*" with absolute certainty. Then you know what all the enlightened masters have known. That is what is called true seeing with no-mind. And what is this no-mind? This very mind: your life and your practice—they are not separate.

We sometimes have the fear that if we really let go of what we are always holding on to, the goal of becoming special, and fully accept that the practice is to be ordinary, then we will lose our drive and determination and finally give up our practice. We actually cling to a deluded goal to maintain our practice! Only when we give up this goal can we see that the practice is my life; I can't give it up, there is no way of stopping. Even if we never sat on a cushion again, practice would go on. How can we give up our very lives? Life and practice are one, on the cushion and off the cushion.

If I gave up sitting now and took up swimming again, still I would be the same person, none the worse for it. But with that kind of open attitude, there is no way you will stop sitting, either; you can drop the fear that you might stop. With no longer any fear about it, you don't have to sit for a reason or create some purpose or goal to keep you going. Then you can truly just sit or just rest or just clean or just work; you don't have to strive for perfection.

Without striving for perfection when you practice, perfection will become of itself true perfection, meaning the absolute perfection that goes beyond relative perfection, that includes imperfection. It includes all your moods: when you are sad, being sad; when you are lonely, being completely lonely; when you are happy, being completely happy. What is so hard about that? We just have to let go of all our *shoulds* and *shouldn'ts*.

> *To live in this faith is the road to nonduality,*
> *because the non-dual is one with the trusting mind.*

In the beginning of practice the most important thing is faith, in the middle the most important thing is faith, in the end the most important thing is faith. To live in this faith is to live a nondual life, to live nondually means to live in this faith. What we call faith doesn't mean faith in some particular person or thing. Our faith in no-thing is more like trust or courage, the courage to overcome fear, to put ourselves wholeheartedly into whatever we do. When the time comes to do some work or chore, it becomes play when we can put ourselves completely into it, giving ourselves away to it with our whole heart. To be one with whatever we are doing, to live nondualistically, means freedom from fear and suffering.

The functioning of the nondual life is compassion. When you really live in nonduality, then why would you try to hurt someone else? It would be like cutting off your own arms or legs. If you really have to amputate, you amputate, but you do not go around intentionally hurting parts of your body unnecessarily.

> *Words!*
> *The Way is beyond language,*
> *for in it there is*
>> *no yesterday*
>> *no tomorrow*
>> *no today.*

Don't get stuck in words and concepts. I have to use words when I give talks, but don't attach to these words. Let them go as fast as they come in. If the words spark something in you, fine; if not, also fine. Either way, don't hold on to them. When I ask students how the talk was, anything they particularly liked about it, and they say they can't remember, that is perfectly OK. I never remember either. I remember only the feeling that I liked it or not, but never the words. I just let the words pass through me like the wind blowing through the clear and empty sky.

Text of the Hsin Hsin Ming
Verses on the Faith Mind
by Sosan Zenji, Third Zen Patriarch

The Great Way is not difficult
for those who have no preferences.
When love and hate are both absent
everything becomes clear and undisguised.
Make the smallest distinction, however,
and heaven and earth are set infinitely apart.
If you wish to see the truth
then hold no opinions for or against anything.
To set up what you like against what you dislike
is the disease of the mind.
When the deep meaning of things is not understood
the mind's essential peace is disturbed to no avail.

The Way is perfect like vast space
where nothing is lacking and nothing is in excess.
Indeed, it is due to our choosing to accept or reject
that we do not see the true nature of things.
Live neither in the entanglements of outer things,
nor in the inner feeling of emptiness.
Be serene in the oneness of things
and such erroneous views will disappear by themselves.
When you try to stop activity to achieve passivity
your very effort fills you with activity.
As long as you remain in one extreme or the other,
you will never know Oneness.

Based upon a translation from the Chinese by Richard B. Clarke

Those who do not live in the single Way
fail in both activity and in passivity,
assertion and denial.
To deny the reality of things
is to miss their reality;
to assert the emptiness of things
is to miss their reality.
The more you talk and think about it,
the further astray you wander from the truth.
Stop talking and thinking
and there is nothing you will not be able to know.
To return to the root is to find the meaning,
but to pursue appearances is to miss the source.
At the moment of inner enlightenment,
there is a going beyond appearance and emptiness.
The changes that appear to occur in the empty world
we call real only because of our ignorance.
Do not search for the truth;
only cease to cherish opinions.

Do not remain in the dualistic state;
avoid such pursuits carefully.
If there is even a trace
of this and that, of right and wrong,
the Mind-essence will be lost in confusion.
Although all dualities come from the One,
do not be attached even to this One.
When the mind exists undisturbed in the Way,
nothing in the world can offend,
and when a thing can no longer offend,
it ceases to exist in the old way.

When no discriminating thoughts arise,
the old mind ceases to exist.
When thought objects vanish,
the thinking-subject vanishes,
as when the mind vanishes, objects vanish.
Things are objects because there is a subject or mind;

and the mind is a subject because there are objects.
Understand the relativity of these two
and the basic reality: the unity of emptiness.
In this Emptiness the two are indistinguishable
and each contains in itself the whole world.
If you do not discriminate between coarse and fine
you will not be tempted to prejudice and opinion.

To live in the Great Way
is neither easy nor difficult.
But those with limited views
are fearful and irresolute:
the faster they hurry, the slower they go.
Clinging cannot be limited;
even to be attached to the idea of enlightenment
is to go astray.
Just let things be in their own way
and there will be neither coming nor going.

Obey the nature of things
and you will walk freely and undisturbed.
When thought is in bondage the truth is hidden,
for everything is murky and unclear.
The burdensome practice of judging
brings annoyance and weariness.
What benefit can be derived
from distinctions and separations?

If you wish to move in the One Way
do not dislike even the world of senses and ideas.
Indeed, to accept them fully
is identical with true Enlightenment.
The wise man strives to no goals
but the foolish man fetters himself.
There is one Dharma, not many;
distinctions arise from the clinging needs of the ignorant.
To seek Mind with discriminating mind
is the greatest of all mistakes.

Rest and unrest derive from illusion;
with enlightenment there is no liking and disliking.
All dualities come from ignorant inference.
They are like dreams of flowers in air:
foolish to try to grasp them.
Gain and loss, right and wrong:
such thoughts must finally be abolished at once.

If the eye never sleeps,
all dreams will naturally cease.
If the mind makes no discriminations,
the ten thousand things
are as they are, of single essence.
To understand the mystery of this One-essence
is to be released from all entanglements.
When all things are seen equally
the timeless Self-essence is reached.
No comparisons or analogies are possible
in this causeless, relationless state.

Consider motion in stillness
and stillness in motion,
both movement and stillness disappear.
When such dualities cease to exist
Oneness itself cannot exist.
To this ultimate finality
no law or description applies.

For the unified mind in accord with the Way
all self-centered striving ceases.
Doubts and irresolutions vanish
and life in true faith is possible.
With a single stroke we are freed from bondage;
nothing clings to us and we hold to nothing.
All is empty, clear, self-illuminating,
with no exertion of the mind's power.
Here thought, feeling, knowledge, and imagination are of
    no value.

In this world of Suchness
there is neither self nor other-than-self.

To come directly into harmony with this reality
just simply say when doubt arises, "Not two."
In this "not two" nothing is separate,
nothing is excluded.
No matter when or where,
enlightenment means entering this truth.
And this truth is beyond extension or diminution in time
    or space;
in it a single thought is ten thousand years.

Emptiness here, Emptiness there,
but the infinite universe stands
always before your eyes.
Infinitely large and infinitely small;
no difference, for definitions have vanished
and no boundaries are seen.
So too with Being and non-Being.
Don't waste time in doubts and arguments
that have nothing to do with this.

One thing, all things:
move among and intermingle,
without distinction.
To live in this realization
is to be without anxiety about nonperfection.
To live in this faith is the road to nonduality,
because the nondual is one with the trusting mind.

Words!
The Way is beyond language,
for in it there is
    no yesterday
    no tomorrow
    no today.

GLOSSARY

ANUTTARA SAMYAK SAMBODHI (Skt.) Supreme complete awakening.

ARHAT (Skt.) *Arhat* or *arahant* was originally a title given to people of high spiritual achievement. It was applied by the early Buddhists to one who had eliminated all defilements and had "no more to learn." *Arhat* practice was later contrasted with the Bodhisattva's way, in which emphasis is on compassion for others.

AVALOKITESVARA *See* KANZEON.

AVATAMSAKA SUTRA (Skt.; Chin. *Hua-yen ching*; Jap. *Kegon kyo*) Literally, "garland sutra," the *Avatamsaka Sutra* is said to be the teachings of Shakyamuni Buddha during the three weeks immediately following his great enlightenment. It expounds the mutual interdependence and interpenetration of all phenomena and is the basic text of the Hua-yen school.

BANKEI YOTAKU (1622–1693) A very popular teacher who taught, in direct and simple language, that we are already the unborn Buddha-mind.

BASO (709–788) One of the most outstanding Zen teachers, especially noted for his use of numerous training methods. He had 139 successors and is famous for many sayings and incidents now incorporated into case koans.

BODHI-MIND The mind in which an aspiration to enlightenment has been awakened.

BODHIDHARMA (Skt.; Jap. Daruma; d. 532) The twenty-eighth Dharma descendant of Shakyamuni Buddha, Bodhidharma was the Indian master who brought Zen to China, where he became known as the First Patriarch. According to tradition he sat in a cave for nine years before transmitting the Dharma to Hui-k'o (Jap. Eka), the Second Patriarch in China (see the *Mumonkan*, Case 41). Attributed to Bodhidharma is the famous four-line verse characterizing Zen:

> A special transmission outside the scriptures
> No dependence on words or letters.

Seeing directly into the mind of man
Realizing true nature, becoming Buddha.

BODHISATTVA (Skt.) Literally, "enlightenment being"; one who practices the Buddha Way and compassionately forgoes final enlightenment for the sake of helping others become enlightened; the exemplar in Mahayana Buddhism.

BUDDHA (Skt.) Literally, "awakened one"; a term that variously indicates the historical Buddha, Shakyamuni; enlightened persons who have attained buddhahood; and the essential truth, the true nature of all beings. *See* BUDDHA-NATURE and SHAKYAMUNI.

BUDDHADHARMA (Jap. *buppo*) The true realization of life; the Way to follow in order to attain that realization according to the teachings of Shakyamuni Buddha.

BUDDHA-MIND *See* BODHI-MIND.

BUDDHA-NATURE The intrinsic nature of all beings; true nature, true self.

DAI KENSHO (Jap.) This term refers to great enlightenment or the "Great Death" experience, seeing completely into one's true nature beyond all doubt. *See* KENSHO.

DAISAN (Jap.) A one-to-one encounter between a Zen student and a sensei in which the student's understanding is probed and stimulated and in which the student may consult the teacher on any matters arising directly out of practice.

DAI SHIN (Jap.) Great heart or mind, sometimes called Big Mind, where one is not functioning out of ego-centeredness.

DANA PARAMITA (Skt.) *See* PARAMITAS.

DHARMA (Skt.) The teachings of Shakyamuni Buddha; Truth; Buddhist doctrine; universal law.

DHARMA COMBAT A lively interchange in which two Zen students, or student and teacher, test and sharpen their understanding.

DHARMAKAYA (Skt.; Jap. *hosshin*) First of three aspects of Buddhanature, known as the three bodies. *Dharmakaya* indicates the absolute beyond all discrimination; the inexpressible truth and transcendental reality; the unity of Buddha with all beings. The second aspect, *sambhogakaya*, refers to the Buddhas who manifest the powers arising from perfect enlightenment. The third, *nirmanakaya*, is Buddha-nature in human form acting for the benefit of sentient beings.

DHARMAS (Skt.) Phenomena; elements or constituents of existence.

DHARMA TALK *See* TEISHO.

DIAMOND SUTRA (Skt. *Vajracchedika Sutra*; Jap. *Kongo kyo*) A text highly regarded by the Zen sect, it sets forth the doctrines of *shunyata* and *prajna* (q.v.). The Sixth Patriarch attained enlightenment upon hearing a phrase from this sutra.

DOGEN KIGEN ZENJI (1200–1253) After training for nine years under the Rinzai, Dogen Zenji made the difficult journey to China, where he studied with and became Dharma successor to T'ien-t'ung Ju-ching (Jap. Tendo Nyojo) in the Soto Zen lineage. Considered the founder of the Japanese Soto school, Dogen Zenji established Eiheiji, the principal Soto training monastery, and is best known for his collection of Dharma essays, *Shobogenzo* (q.v.).

DOJO (Jap.) A training place.

DOKUSAN (Jap.) A one-to-one encounter between a Zen student and a roshi in which the student's understanding is probed and stimulated and in which the student may consult the teacher on any matters arising directly out of practice.

DUHKHA (Skt.) The First Noble Truth taught by Shakyamuni Buddha. It refers to our basic dissatisfaction, suffering, alienation, and loneliness; to our not being at peace. The Second Noble Truth identifies the cause of this suffering as our craving and despising, attachments and aversions, due to our ignorance. The Third Noble Truth states that liberation from all clinging brings about complete peace, *nirvana*. The Fourth Noble Truth is the Eightfold Path that leads to this liberation. *See* EIGHTFOLD PATH; NIRVANA.

EIGHTFOLD PATH The Fourth Noble Truth, in which Shakyamuni Buddha indicated the Way to put an end to suffering. The Eightfold Path consists of right views, right thought, right speech, right action, right livelihood, right effort, right mindfulness, and right *samadhi*.

EKA The Japanese name of the Second Patriarch Hui-k'o, who received the Dharma transmission from Bodhidharma and passed it on to Sosan (Chin. Seng-ts'an), the Third Patriarch, to whom the *Hsin hsin ming* is attributed. Eka is famous for his unstoppable determination to be Bodhidharma's student. When he implored Bodhidharma to pacify his mind, Bodhidharma asked Eka to show him this mind. When Eka returned after ten days of unceasing effort and asserted that he definitely could not find his mind, Bodhidharma confirmed that his mind had now been pacified.

EMPTINESS (Skt. *shunyata*) The fundamental nature of all phenomena.

ENYADATTA (Skt.) A character in a story told by Shakyamuni Buddha in the *Lotus Sutra*. Enyadatta thought she had lost her head and searched frantically to find it, refusing to believe she still had it.

Enyadatta's search for her head represents the Zen student's seeking after his or her true nature. (See chapter 6 for a more detailed account of the story.)

FOUR VOWS "Sentient beings are numberless; I vow to save them. Desires are inexhaustible; I vow to put an end to them. The Dharmas are boundless; I vow to master them. The Buddha Way is unsurpassable; I vow to attain it." Zen students chant these vows daily as an expression of their aspiration.

GANTO (828–887) One of Tokusan's successors and a close Dharma brother of Seppo. Ganto's great shout as he died became an important koan for many who followed, including the great master Hakuin Zenji.

GASSHO (Jap.) Literally, "palms of the hands placed together"; a gesture of respect that expresses unity of being.

GREAT DEATH *See* DAI KENSHO.

HAKUIN EKAKU ZENJI (1686–1769) The Patriarch of Japanese Rinzai Zen, through whom all present-day Rinzai masters have their lineage. He systematized koan study as we know it today and is known for his drawings and paintings, especially of Bodhidharma.

HARA (Jap.) The area of the lower abdomen that is the physical center of gravity of the human body. The *hara* becomes a center of awareness in zazen.

HOSSHIN *See* DHARMAKAYA.

HYAKUJO (720–814) Hyakujo laid down rules of conduct for monks in Zen monasteries. He was the teacher of Obaku, who was Rinzai's teacher.

IDENTITY OF RELATIVE AND ABSOLUTE (Jap. *Sandokai*) One of the most important Zen poems, this profound sutra is chanted daily in Soto Zen services.

INDRA'S NET This image from the *Avatamsaka Sutra* pictures a cosmic net with a jewel at every intersection. All the jewels reflect each other. Just as one jewel contains all others, every moment of awareness contains the unity, the diversity, and the interrelatedness of all. *See* AVATAMSAKA SUTRA.

INKA (Jap.) The special seal of approval given to highly accomplished Dharma successors who have completed koan study and have attained the maturity to guide students in koan study as well as in the practice of zazen.

JORIKI (Jap.) Literally, "*samadhi* power"; the vital, stabilizing energy arising from strong zazen practice. *See* SAMADHI.

JUKAI (Jap.) The ceremony of receiving the precepts. One who receives the precepts formally becomes a Buddhist and is given a Dharma name. *See* PRECEPTS.

KANZEON (Jap. also *Kannon*, or *Kan Ji Sai Bosa*; Skt. *Avalokitesvara*; Chin. *Kuan-yin*) Literally, "the one who hears the sounds and cries (or supplications) of the world"; Kanzeon is one of the principal Bodhisattvas in the Zen Buddhist tradition, personifying great compassion. While usually represented in the female form, Kanzeon traditionally manifested in whatever form was needed in order to answer the needs of beings. In Genpo Sensei's words, Kanzeon stands for the compassion, the love, the mercy within each one of us.

KARMA (Skt.) The principle of causality, which holds that for every effect there is a cause and, in the human sphere, maintains that by our actions we determine the quality of our lives and influence the lives of others.

KEIZAN JOKIN ZENJI (1268–1325) A Japanese Zen master who became a monk under Dogen Zenji's disciple Koun Ejo. He founded a number of monasteries throughout Japan including Sojiji, one of the two primary Soto Zen monasteries in Japan today. He was the Fourth Patriarch of Japanese Soto Zen and the most important after Dogen Zenji.

KENSHO (Jap.) Literally, "seeing into one's nature"; an experience of enlightenment. Also known as *satori*.

KINHIN (Jap.) Walking zazen, usually done for five or ten minutes between periods of sitting zazen.

KOAN (Jap.; Chin. *kung-an*) Literally, "public document"; in the Zen tradition, a statement, question, anecdote, or dialogue that cannot be understood or resolved intellectually. Meditation on a koan leads one to transcend the intellect and experience the nondual nature of reality. Koans are given by the Zen teacher to bring students to realization and to help them clarify their understanding. Approximately seventeen hundred koans have been recorded from Chinese and Japanese sources. Many of these recount an exchange between master and student or a master's enlightenment experience and are known as "case koans." They can be found in various collections, most notably *The Gateless Gate (Mumonkan)*, *The Blue Cliff Record (Hekigan roku)*, *The Book of Equanimity (Shoyo roku)*, and *The Book of the Transmission of the Lamp (Denko roku)*. *See* KOAN STUDY.

KOAN STUDY The intensive, nonintellectual study of koans in Zen meditation. Conventional discursive thinking is bypassed and a student is encouraged to give spontaneous, direct responses that express the heart of the matter in question. Koan study helps a student learn the structure of the Dharma and sharpens his or her *prajna. See* KOAN; PRAJNA.

KODO SAWAKI ROSHI (1880–1965) A famous Soto Zen monk who shunned any form of institutional practice and who never had his own temple. He traveled extensively throughout Japan teaching zazen.

KORYU OSAKA ROSHI (d. 1985) A Japanese Rinzai Zen master from whom Maezumi Roshi, Genpo Sensei's teacher, received *inka* in 1972.

MANJUSHRI (Skt.; Jap. Monju) The Bodhisattva of wisdom, often depicted riding a lion and holding a sword of wisdom that cuts through delusion. Especially appreciated in the Zen sect, Manjushri Bodhisattva is the principal figure on the zendo altar.

MU (Jap., or *muji*) The character *mu* is a negative particle used in Zen to point directly at reality and has no discursive content. The use of the word in this sense originated with Joshu Jushin (Chin. Chao-chou Ts'ung-shen, 778–897) who, when asked by a monk, "Does a dog have Buddha-nature?," directly answered, "*Mu!*" This incident is used as the opening koan in *The Gateless Gate* and is often the first koan encountered by Zen students in their koan study. The term *mu* is often used as a synonym for *emptiness* (q.v.).

MUMON EKAI (1183–1260) A student of Master Getsurin Shikan; after six years of working on Joshu's *Mu*, Mumon experienced *dai kensho* upon hearing the sound of a drum. He produced the koan collection best known in the West, *The Gateless Gate (Mumonkan)*, in which the first koan is Joshu's *Mu. See* DAI KENSHO; KOAN; MU; MUMONKAN.

MUMONKAN (Jap.) *The Gateless Gate*, a major collection of koans consisting of forty-eight cases. *See* KOAN; MUMON EKAI.

NASRUDIN, MULLAH A legendary figure, sage, and fool, originating in stories circulating in the Middle East as early as the twelfth century. The sayings and doings of Mullah Nasrudin have a characteristically ironic and down-to-earth humor.

NIRVANA (Skt.; Jap. *nehan*) A nondualistic state beyond life and death. The original meaning of the term was "to extinguish or burn out because of lack of fuel," implying the complete exhaustion of all ignorance and craving. Extinction or burning out here conveys the sense of space being completely clear, no longer full of clouds and smoke. *Nirvana* sometimes refers specifically to the state of profound enlightenment attained by Shakyamuni Buddha.

NOBLE TRUTHS, FOUR *See* DUHKHA; EIGHTFOLD PATH.

PARAMITAS (Skt.) Literally, "gone to the other shore"; this term refers to the Six Perfections practiced by a Bodhisattva, culminating with *prajna paramita* ("perfection of wisdom"), which informs and fulfills the other five. The *paramitas* are a natural expression of the enlightened mind, the mind of meditation. The six *paramitas* are giving (*dana*), precepts or morality (*sila*), patience (*kshanti*), effort or vigor (*virya*), meditation (*dhyana*), and wisdom (*prajna*). Four more are sometimes added: skillfulness in means (*upaya*), determination (*pranidhana*), strength (*bala*), and knowledge (*jnana*).

PATRIARCH Strictly speaking, this title is given to the first thirty-four Dharma successors from Shakyamuni Buddha through the Sixth Patriarch, Hui-neng (Jap. Eno, 638–713). More generally, it is an honorific term used to describe a Zen master of outstanding attainment.

PRAJNA (Skt.; Jap. *hannya*) Enlightened wisdom; wisdom that transcends duality of subject and object.

PRECEPTS (Skt. *sila*; Jap. *kai*) Buddhist teachings regarding personal conduct, which can be appreciated on a fairly literal level as ethical guidelines and more broadly as aspects or qualities of reality itself. At the time of *jukai*, the Zen practitioner receives and promises to maintain the following precepts. The Three Treasures: be one with the Buddha; be one with the Dharma; be one with the Sangha. The Three Pure Precepts: do not commit evil; do good; do good for others. The Ten Grave Precepts: do not kill; do not steal; do not be greedy; do not tell a lie; do not be ignorant; do not talk about others' faults; do not elevate yourself by criticizing others; do not be stingy; do not get angry; do not speak ill of the Three Treasures. *See* JUKAI.

RINZAI GIGEN (Chin. Lin-chi I-hsuan, d. 866) Rinzai was one of the great masters of the T'ang dynasty in China and the founder of the Rinzai school of Zen, noted for its emphasis on enlightenment and for its vigorous use of koans in zazen practice. Rinzai was a Dharma successor of Obaku Kiun (Chin. Huang-po Hsi-yun).

ROSHI (Jap.) Meaning literally "old teacher"; an honorific term used to refer to a Zen master.

RYUTAN SOSHIN (Chin. Lung-t'an) A great Zen master of the ninth century.

SAMADHI (Skt.; Jap. *zammai*) A state of mind characterized by one-pointedness of attention; a nondualistic state of awareness.

SAMSARA (Skt.) Literally, "stream of becoming"; the experience of suffering arising from ignorance, as set forth in Buddha's Second

Noble Truth. *Samsara* is reflected in the condition of our usual daily life, in which the main focus is perpetuation of a separate self (ego). *See* DUHKHA.

SAMU (Jap.) Working zazen, often indoor or outdoor physical labor.

SANGHA (Skt.) Originally referring to the community of Buddhist monks and nuns, the term *Sangha* later came to include laypersons as well. In Zen, the term also connotes the harmonious interrelationship of all beings, phenomena, and events; in other words, the inseparability and harmonious working of Buddhadharma.

SENSEI (Jap.) Title meaning "teacher."

SENZAKI (d. 1958) One of the pioneering Zen teachers in the West, Nyogen Senzaki lived in Los Angeles from 1905 until his death.

SEPPO (822–908) Zen master, a successor of Tokusan and Dharma brother of Ganto (q.v.).

SESSHIN (Jap.) Literally, "to collect or regulate the mind"; a Zen meditation retreat conventionally lasting seven days.

SHAKYAMUNI (Skt.) Literally, "the sage of the Shakya clan"; this title is used to refer to Siddhartha Gautama, the historical Buddha, after his enlightenment.

SHIKANTAZA (Jap.) Literally, "just sitting"; refers to zazen itself, without supportive devices such as breath-counting or koan study. Characterized by intense nondiscursive awareness, *shikantaza* is "zazen doing zazen for the sake of zazen."

SHOBO (Jap.) A term meaning "the true Dharma."

SHOBOGENZO (Jap.) "Treasury of the True Dharma Eye," the masterwork of Dogen Zenji, founder of the Japanese Soto school of Zen, it comprises some ninety-five articles dealing with a wide variety of Buddhist topics and is generally considered to be one of the most subtle and profound works in Buddhist literature.

SHUNYATA (Skt.) See EMPTINESS.

SIXTH PATRIARCH (Chin. Hui-neng; Jap. Eno, 638–713) Traditionally said to have been illiterate, Hui-neng was enlightened while still a layman upon hearing a recitation of the *Diamond Sutra*. He became a Dharma successor of the Fifth Patriarch, Hung-jen, and all lines of Zen now existing descend from him. His teaching, as recorded in the *Platform Sutra*, stresses "sudden enlightenment" (as opposed to the "gradual enlightenment" of the Northern School of Ch'an, or Zen) and the identity of meditation (*dhyana*) and wisdom (*prajna*). He was largely responsible for the widespread flourishing of Zen in the T'ang dynasty.

SOTO SCHOOL   The Zen lineage founded by Zen masters Tung-shan Liang-chieh (Jap. Tozan Ryokai, 807–869) and Ts'ao-shan Pen-chi (Jap. Sozen Honjaku, 840–901). The Japanese branch was founded by Zen masters Dogen Kigen (1200–1253) and Keizan Jokin (1268–1325).

SOYEN SHAKU ROSHI (1859–1919)   The first Zen master to take an active role in bringing the teaching of Zen to the United States. He was the teacher of Nyogen Senzaki and D. T. Suzuki and had a strong influence on many who were involved in spreading the Dharma in the West early in this century.

SUTRA (Skt.)   Literally, "a thread on which jewels are strung"; a Buddhist scripture. Sutras are the purported dialogues and sermons of Shakyamuni Buddha and of certain other Buddhist figures.

SUZUKI, D. T. (1870–1966)   Daisetz Teitaro Suzuki was for a long time one of the best known and most widely read interpreters of Zen in the West. He had undertaken some lay Zen training and also had deep sympathy with the Shin Buddhist faith. He specialized in the intellectual interpretation of Zen teachings and Mahayana sutras.

TAO (Chin.)   Literally, the "Way," or "Path," Tao is used to indicate Buddha-nature or the Way of or to enlightenment. Since Zen is a marriage between Indian Buddhism and Chinese Taoism, the term is historically significant.

TEISHO (Jap.)   A formal commentary by a Zen master on a koan or other Zen text. In its strictest sense, a *teisho* is nondualistic, which distinguishes it from an ordinary discursive lecture on some Buddhist topic. In this book, the term *Dharma talk* is used synonymously with *teisho*.

TOKUSAN (Jap.; Chin. Te-shan Hsuan-chien; 781?–867)   A most influential teacher, from whom nine major Zen masters received Dharma transmission. After living for a long time in seclusion, Tokusan became famous for the compassionate severity of his training. "Thirty blows if you speak, thirty blows if you do not!"

VIMALAKIRTI (Skt.)   The central character in the *Vimalakirtinirdesa Sutra*, an important Mahayana text, whose spiritual attainment as a layman went beyond all others, including all the great Bodhisattvas. He embodies the Mahayana acceptance that what matters most in practice is not exclusive to those who are ordained, and his silence questions the value of verbal eloquence in expressing *satori*. Vimalakirti wholly identifies himself with the sickness and suffering of beings, taking their sickness upon himself. He teaches Manjushri, the Bodhisattva of wisdom, that the Bodhisattva loves all beings as if each were his only child: he is sick when they are sick and cured when they are cured.

WU, EMPEROR   When Bodhidharma first arrived in China, he was invited to the Buddhist Emperor Wu's court. Much to the emperor's regret ever afterward, he did not realize who Bodhidharma was and could not grasp the significance of his teaching (*Blue Cliff Record*, Case 1). Later on, after Bodhidharma had departed, Emperor Wu's daughter was sent by her father to study with him, and she became one of his four major disciples.

YIN/YANG (Chin.)   In Taoist philosophy, the two polar energies. The interaction of yin and yang is the source of the universe. *Yin* refers to the feminine, passive, receptive, dark, and soft aspects and *yang* to the masculine, active, creative, bright, and hard.

ZAZEN (Jap.)   *Za* is "sitting," and *zen* is *samadhi*. *Zazen* connotes the practice of meditation in Zen that contains both these elements. Neither sitting nor concentration, however, encompasses the whole of zazen, of which it is said by Hakuin Zenji, "No praise can exhaust its merits," and by Dogen Zenji, "The Way of the Buddhas and Patriarchs is nothing but zazen. Do not pursue anything else."

ZEN (Jap.)   A school of Buddhism whose main emphasis is zazen or sitting meditation. The word *Zen* is the Japanese rendering of the Chinese *ch'an*, which comes from the Sanskrit *dhyana*, meaning "meditation" or "concentration." Here *Zen* indicates meditation in all its aspects rather than simply concentration, or *samadhi*.

ZENDO (Jap.)   A place set aside for the practice of zazen.

ZENJI (Jap.)   Literally, "Zen master"; an honorific term used to refer to a master of high rank or attainment.